# WHEN SCHOOL STARTS SUCKING

# WHEN SCHOOL STARTS SUCKING

MOHIT PRIYADARSHI

PUBLICATIONS

KALPAZ PUBLICATIONS

DELHI-110052

When School Starts Sucking



ISBN: 81-7835-638-4



Published in 2008 in India by
Kalpaz Publications
C-30, Satyawati Nagar,
Delhi-110052
E-mail: kalpaz@hotmail.com
Phone : 9212729499

*Laser Type Setting by*: Rudra Computer Graphics, Delhi
Printed by : Vishal Kaushik Printer's, Delhi

*In Dedication to*
*My Grandma and Grandpa*

# Contents

Acknowledgments

Just as every author does before starting his book, I would like to thank a number of people without whom the completion of this book would've been a mere dream. Firstly, I'll thank my parents for all the support they provided me. They were my first readers and of course, the first critics. Then, I would thank my sisters who have been very kind throughout, more eager than me to write off a good book. Thank you, Manisha, Sweta and Divya didi for what you provided to your young brother.

Most importantly, I'll want to thank all my friends for the pleasure that they've bestowed to me during all the time that they've stayed with me. You guys made my life rocking! A BIG THANKS to all of you-Prashant, Gautam, Shishir, Shivam, Shashank, Kishore, Malay, Vivek, Revant, Pushp, Rajeev, Abhinav, Sameer, Arshit, Satyam, Mayank, Aditya (and of course their girlfriends because they provided me with the other side of their two-way personality) and anyone and everyone that has had an impact on my life. I'm extremely regretful if I've missed someone.

I'll thank all my girl classmates separately because of the adorable time that they provided me at my sucking school. Girls, if it wasn't for your beautiful faces that kept my eyes glued on you, my school life might have been a lot worse.

Also, I would thank one of my English teachers, Mrs. Archana Jha, for improving my English up to such a level that I could convert my life into words. Maybe you don't know ma'am, but your teaching way was lovable. I don't know where you are presently, but wherever you are, thanks yet again.

And at last I would like to thank God, it has been because of him that a desire of writing a book sprang into my mind.

# Prologue

This is my book. Yeah, I think I've every right to call this book mine though there are loads of other people who helped me in composing this experience. This piece is entirely my perspective of how I live my life along with my friends. You would think what was so forceful in my life that it appealed to me to write a complete book. But I'll tell you what: the experience is worth mentioning. However, whether it is as significant as spending more than two hundred hours in front of my computer (since I used Microsoft Word), you decide.

Primarily, there are two reasons that compelled me to express my experiences in such a way. First of all, I want you to realize that it's not easy being an average student in India. It's a hell lot difficult to prepare for the competitive exams along with your Boards. And there are pupils who get torn apart because of such a system. I, myself, am a leading example.

Secondly, I would also tell you that how students lead their lives pleasurably even with so much pressure on them to perform. It is this time that we identify our friends, and of course we find out our real identity. Maybe students like me don't build the greatest of futures for themselves, but then we know what we are doing and what way we should live. This book contains my three-night stay at my friend's home, and it is one of the two reasons that I compiled this tome. The time I spent there was simply unforgettable, and also enjoyable at the highest degree.

And it is this time of our life that the school starts sucking. School life is so much fun when you are a kid, and it's worst when you are in high school. Maybe your school life wasn't as miserable, but don't forget it is my experience that we are talking about. The schools have a simple ambition set for themselves-they want their students to be the best, to get the highest marks. However, the way the pupils get to that level doesn't matter to them. They want to produce intellectual students from their school because it is by doing this that they acquire high reputation and publicity.

Just before I start my lecture though, I would like you to understand that friendship for me is the best invention man has done since his genesis on this planet. Friendship merely doesn't mean helping each other in times of need, it means understanding each other's soul. I most certainly wouldn't go into deeper interpretations since I'm the worst philosopher on earth. I don't know if this book will deliver what you expect, but I assure you this will help you recognizing life better and how to live it. So enjoy your stay with me and my friends.... or at least try to enjoy.

# 1

# Pranav's Proposal

So, let me first introduce you to my friends. There is of course the all important Pranav-I call him important because it was his home where we did all the drama (referring to three night-stay of course). Then, there is Raj who according to me is the coolest guy I've met all my life. His presence surely made the nights wonderful. There are two other dudes who marked their presence in style: Zayed and Ravi. Neither of them stayed at Pranav's place all three nights, but even their small participation was enough to create unlimited fun.

I won't go in much detail about explaining each of their personalities but certainly would give you some inputs as for you to understand the plot better. Pranav is a good-looking decent human being who tries to make things simple at the outset. I have known him only for six months but our bond has been strong from the very beginning. Raj, as I already mentioned, is a superb entertainer with his humorous jokes and uncanny ideas. As far as sophistication is considered in our gang, Zayed is the one to look out for. He has a ready-to-hit-you-if-you-come-in-my-way attitude but can do anything for his friends. Last but not the least, Ravi is there. A remarkable fan of Shahrukh Khan, he copies his personality traits to make himself noticed. Nonetheless, he is a champion material.

Okay, enough introductions. As the story progresses, more characters may join in. Here is where the story begins:

'Give me any new DVDs if you have, we will be watching them during the time Raj stays at my place' Pranav said in a low but clear voice.

'Huh?' I responded as I was busy searching my mobile for new messages.

'Oh, I forgot to tell you. Mummy and Daddy are going to grandma's place for four days and I asked Raj if he could spend the nights at my home during their visit. Can you?' added Pranav.

'And what did Raj say?' I interrogated.

'He said he would ask his parents. Though I feel he will get their nod. Will your parents allow?'

'I dunno... such situations have never occurred. Let's see. Why are your parents going anyway?' I asked.

'Some puja is taking place at Grandma's home.'

'And you are not going?'

'No, not at all. I can't afford to miss my tuitions' he said.

'Oh, great. Here lies the irony. You won't go to the puja because you will miss classes and now here you are at my home playing computer games bunking your math tuition' I said proudly at having created the ironical situation.

'Aaahhh! Sinha is boring anyway. Further, I don't understand a word he teaches. By the way, Harsh was asking when he should arrange the next football match' Pranav said.

'Any day that pleases him and other mates. Friday or Saturday would be both fine.'

'Will Rebu be able to come?' asked Pranav. Rebu was our star footballer. He was certainly the best in our group at playing soccer.

'Not sure, though he cherishes every chance of playing at Gandhi Maidan. I'll ask him or rather persuade him to come. All right?' I asked.

'Okay. Saturday would be better. Rebu would have school on Friday' said Pranav. It's not that we don't study at school; it's only that our school sometimes gave vacations unnecessarily (we enjoyed them a lot though).

'Absolutely. I'll talk to papa about staying at your place' I said.

'Try your level best. Gotta go, dude' he said, picked his bag and moved towards the door.

'Bye.'

'Good night.'

# 2

# Next Day at School

I woke up next morning with dreams of terrible teachers still haunting me. I didn't want to go to the school one bit but the thoughts of meeting my friends encouraged me. I had not discussed Pranav's proposal with papa yet but was hopeful of him giving me permission. So, finally I was in standard XII... I dreamt of being the hunk at high school since my childhood but was nowhere near it. Anyways, the clock showed seven and I had to be at school by eight.

'C'mon, Arjun. Be fast. You would be late for your school' said mummy and removed the thin bed sheet covering me.

This... yes, this was the part I hated. I loathed waking up from my bed. Yet, I had to. I couldn't afford to miss my first day of class XII.

'You get the coffee ready and I would be there in five minutes' I said.

'And how have you thought of going to school today?' mummy questioned.

'Why? The car is in a perfect shape and it does have enough petrol to reach the boring place' I answered. You guessed it right. I often refer to my school as the most *boring place.*

Within ten minutes I was there at the table where the coffee was already waiting. I often wonder how mummies could be so fast. They have loads of other jobs and still they take care of their offspring like no one else can. I drank the coffee in two gulps with a couple of biscuits and quickly ran towards the bathroom for a sharp shower.

'Ready?' mummy asked as I shut the door and moved towards the portico where the car was parked. She was plucking flowers of a tree which was her favourite morning past-time.

'Yep, I'm ready' I said and unlocked the car.

'Give me the keys, Arjun' mummy said.

'No ways, I'll drive' I retaliated and sat on the driver's seat.

Mummy did not protest. She did not enjoy my rash driving but was always up for the challenge. But as far as driving was concerned, I loved it.

'Which section are you expecting?' mummy asked as I swiftly took the turn towards Bailey Road. Okay, I'll tell you what's all that about. We are divided according to our marks of annual semesters in class XII and considering I hadn't scored huge, I responded.

'I think I would be sent to C or D. Whatever, I want to be with my friends' I said and saw the school bus picking up students at the roundabout.

I did not want to be in A or B which, I was sure, would be filled with muggers and pupils who don't have any work other than preparing for the competitive exams. It's not that I didn't want to crack an exam which would get me into a reputed college; it's only that I was more relaxed.

I stopped the car as I saw a stream of students entering the school campus. Some of them were expressionless; some sad like I was and some filled with enthusiasm. I can't believe people were happy coming to this place.

'Bye, mummy' I said and took my bag from the rear seat.

'Bye, son and have a good day' she said and turned the car as I saw Ravi looking grimly at the notice board.

'So dude, what's up?' I asked at having reached Ravi. I scanned the notice board to find out what was making him look like this. I found nothing important other than the date for the next volleyball trials.

'Oh, hi. I didn't see you coming. I thought they will put the list on the notice board' he said.

'What list? About the new sections?' I inquired.

'Yes. I'm a bit worried about my allocation. I don't think many friends will be around me. You scored in mid seventies, right?' he asked.

'Yep, mid seventies' I responded.

'Everyone in our circle has more or less scored like that. I've only fallen in the sixties. This rule of dividing according to marks sucks' he said.

'Sucking rule of a sucker school. Anyways, don't worry about allocations, we'll be together' I said trying to uplift his mood though I had a serious feeling of him not being with me and other friends.

'Doesn't matter, these rules can't separate us. By the way, that rhymed nicely-SUCKING RULE OF A SUCKER SCHOOL' he added laying extra-emphasis on the last line. Some juniors even turned to see us with a seniors-are-like-that expression on their faces.

'Yeah, that's like a man', I said and gave him a pat on the back ignoring the still-looking school-respecting juniors. 'As far as the rhyming line goes, I must tell you that I wanted to be a poet when I was three, only didn't get the time, you understand?' I continued.

'Of course I do', he said with a wide grin on his face. I was happy at the fact that I had been able to make him feel better. 'I assume that we have to go back to our old sections and we would be told there about where to proceed as this damn notice board has nothing to communicate' he completed.

'Most certainly' I said and went with him to the second floor where the old sections were. He proceeded to his old section and I to mine. We were in separate sections the last year anyway.

As I entered the section, I saw students covering every inch of the room talking among themselves about the criteria of marks on which the division was to take place. Our classroom was quite big with five columns of desks having seven rows each. On ceiling hung the ancient fans which were too tired to provide any kind of respite from the ailing weather. I saw Pranav sitting on the last bench of the third column and moved my feet towards him. Beside him sat Vicky who was an extremely thin but good natured boy who reminded me of malnourished India every time I saw him.

'Hi, so how are you two doing?' I asked as I approached them

'Quite fine', both of them said together. 'Don't discuss anything about the allocations, I have blown my mind talking about it for the last half an hour' Pranav said.

'Good. I don't want to talk about it either. When are your parents leaving? I forgot, when did you say?' I interrogated.

'I hadn't said that to you since you didn't ask me. Anyways, they will leave on next Wednesday and would be back by Saturday. Why? You asked uncle?' he confirmed.

'No, not as yet. We have plenty of time though. Today is only Monday and we have about eight days left. I'll get their permission, I feel' I said.

By this time, Vicky had left us as a boy took him to show a girl they had never previously noticed in the school. Vicky had this strange habit of observing every beautiful girl in the school premises from distance but didn't dare talking to even one of them.

Thinking about girls, Pranav's girlfriend Zeesha came to my mind. I wondered if she could be called his *girlfriend* as they always talked formally and never met outside the *boring place*. It was partly due to the fact that Zeesha lived near Bypass Road which was twenty kilometers away from Pranav's home and partly due to unknown reasons. I figured out the causes quite well, I thought.

'So, how's Zeesha?' I asked.

'She's fine. I haven't talked to her lately but Preeti said she got good marks and is quite content with her performance' he replied. Preeti was Zeesha's closest friend at school and was Pranav's bus-mate.

'That's nice. You expected it from her, eh?' I asked.

'Yeah, quite so. By the way, day before yesterday was her birthday and here is my gift' he said as he took out a packet from his bag. What I saw was an immensely decorated and beautifully wrapped show piece.

'Oh, lovely. This is magnificently packed' I said. I had never given such superbly bedecked gift to anyone and had neither received any. It is just so natural that boys give their non-deserving girlfriends (I didn't know whether it was true for Zeesha) such high esteem and recalled how Pranav had wrapped my gift on my birthday. The consequences of my thoughts were a total contrast.

As we talked further about Zeesha and her present, our class teacher Mr. Varun entered the class. He was one of the worst teachers of the school (there were more bad teachers in this school than good) and had a distinctly bad impression about Pranav and me as we were highly notorious in his classes. Vicky and the other guys were back big time.

'Good morning, class' he said in his high-pitched voice.

'Good morning, sir' half the class responded gloomily.

'So, how are you all doing?' he said as he sat on the teacher's chair.

'Fine, sir' some of the boys chorused in the latest bollywood tune.

'Some of you may remain in this section; some will go to C, some to D and so on. You all will get what you deserve. The good ones will remain in this section and will get good teachers, maybe even me' he said and I couldn't believe he considered himself as a *good* teacher. 'Though wherever you go', he continued, 'try to be the best. We'll be getting the list in about fifteen minutes. See what happens' he said and continued this nuisance lecture till the list arrived.

I was happy to see the allocation list come sooner than later as I couldn't tolerate his disgusting speech.

'First of all, as many of you don't know, Abhijit has topped the class with eighty-nine percent marks', he said and gave an affectionate look to the topper. 'Now, the divisions' he said and read the names of the students along with their new sections. Pranav, Vicky and I were drawn to the same section D.

The XII standard sections were on the first floor and there we proceeded. We went and sat in the empty XII D section and waited to see who else would unite with us in this new place. A couple of our old class-mates Mayank and Shashi didn't join us and I was pondering over it.

Pranav, as if he read my mind, said, 'All our friends can't come to this section, it's impossible. Though I would be satisfied if a couple of them come here.'

'Yes, I agree. Kishore, Rajiv and Ashu may join us. Their marks were close to ours', maybe even Shubham' Vicky said.

Vicky had figured it out quite well. Kishore, Ashu and Rajiv were drawn to D as well and I was pleased to see them. All of them were good lads but it is something about Kishore that I can't express. He has a persona about himself that can't be framed into words. He is always busy in some kind of work but has utmost admiration for his family and friends.

The three of them approached the three of us and we gave each other high fives. We all were content with the divisions and had quite expected it to go the same way. We had known Raj and Zayed wouldn't come here as they scored in the mid sixties. There was a chance for Ravi and Shubham but not now as the entire new section was in front of our eyes.

The six of us sat in the third column with Pranav and me occupying the last bench, Kishore and Rajiv in front of us and Vicky and Ashu further in front. I noticed that the number of girls was almost equal to the number of boys and that satisfied me further.

'So, everyone happy?' I asked in a loud enough voice for the six of us to hear. 'We can't have an entire section full of only our friends' I added.

'Who would be our class teacher? That would be a bit of suspense' Ashu said as all of my friends had already answered my question with there genuine gestures.

'Dunno, hope it is someone caring. I don't want to have a class teacher who screws our last year at school. It would be so much more fun if we didn't have any' Rajiv said and chuckled at the thought of the impossible situation.

Finally, here we were. This was supposed to be our family for the entire year that beckoned us. Now, only the head of the family had to arrive and he did just that. Mr. Lalji Das, one of the few teachers that knew their subjects, was appointed our class teacher. He taught physics and had great command over it. Certainly we were more than happy. I could see a sigh of relief on most of the students' faces.

The rest of the day passed with us noticing the teachers and the teachers noticing us. We, that is, the friends discussed various issues ranging from girls to cricketers to politicians. It would be so wonderful if every day was like this. At the lunch break, we met other pals.

'It's good that I've Zayed with me or the rubbish section would have choked me to death' said Raj in a rough voice as he had his mouth full with Kishore's scrumptious paw-bhaji. Yes, this too added to Kishore's guise. He had the most wonderful tradition of bringing a variety of appetizing dishes.

'And so is the case with me, further we don't have a single girl in our class' said Zayed and put his hands on his eyes to wipe out the imaginary tears. This was the case with my friends-they all had something in common; all of them were brilliant dramatists. It only spiced our flavour of talking.

'It's heartrending. I can't imagine a class without girls, such a pity' I said raising each of my hands to both Raj and Zayed as if trying to console them from the most depressing situation possible in a co-ed school.

'Same is the case with us' said Shubham as he approached us along with Ravi. Of all my friends, Shubham was the most interactive, at least with me. We shared the same choices, same problems and had the same crush. I'll tell you about that later. It's only unfortunate that you won't find much of Shubham in this book as he was not involved with us in our three-night stay. For the reason, read further.

# 3

# Jai's Dilemma

Going by the name of this chapter, you would be speculating about the inclusion of the new character. Listen, most of the characters in this book are my comrades and more or less they are like me. After all, that's why they are my friends. So, don't try to understand each of them, just take pleasure in the narrative.

Tuesday at school was somewhat like the previous day. We were still settling in our new sections. The only development was that I had told papa that I would need the car to leave me at school for this week, as I would be making a cycle pass next Monday or thereabout. We needed to make passes for parking our bicycles in the school grounds.

On Tuesday, I had my chemistry tuition. Ravi, Shubham, Vicky and I were all in the same coaching as well. Here is where you will come across some more dudes. Jai is one of them, with a distinctive individuality. Again, he's tough to explain but is a magician at creating moods. He has something funny to say every nanosecond and that's how he lives his life. Not to mention, he is a magnificent artist and draws beautiful outlines or sketches of cars and bikes. I guess that's the reason why he wants to become an automobile engineer.

Then there is Karan, who according to me is the largest human being you will know in this manuscript. Physically robust and tall, he has some traits of a gang leader but is mellow at heart. It's amazing how the look of an individual may give an entirely wrong impression to the observer.

Also, Naman or the *mugger* as we call him is just the kind of chap you would expect to crack the IITJEE. A contrast of Karan, this thirty kilo dude was thoroughly devoted to his studies. Good, at least someone I know has high ambitions.

The tuition commenced at four in the evening but our teacher used to arrive at least twenty minutes late everyday. So we got plenty of time to discuss diverse matters. Adding to that, our educator was superb in two aspects; first, he taught luminously and second, he was over-indulgent. That did not mean, however, that we didn't pay attention in his classes. We only used to be highly garrulous (girls don't gossip only, boys do it as well).

'Oh God! Don't ask me how much I've wished to get out of the house since yesterday. Mummy has been all over me' Jai said with extreme anxiety, marking his presence.

The *don't ask me* phrase compelled me to ask the question even faster. Well, it is for this reason that people use phrases.

'What's the affair?' I inquired. I tried to keep my tone relaxed but my effort did nothing more than intensifying my angst.

'I told you I called Ankita on Valentine's Day' he said.

'Yep, but it was almost two months back' I interrupted.

'Let him speak' said Shubham and signaled me to keep quiet. I observed that everyone was listening with paramount sincerity. Naman, however, was the exception as you might have already conjectured.

'But I was unable to talk to her as all of you already know' Jai continued, 'I called her again yesterday but she was unavailable. And in the evening, the phone rang and there she was. Ill-fatedly, it was mummy who picked it and she has been thinking all wrong of our friendship since then. All kinds of hullabaloos have overtaken her mind and she isn't ready to listen to me one-bit. Papa isn't here otherwise he might have screwed me further' he completed and saw us with an expression that demanded our valuable comments.

'Okay, that's the case. What fuss has been aunty thinking of?' Shubham quizzed.

'What not? She has been thinking that I've shared some kind of a relationship with her but she doesn't know we have always talked occasionally. She has made me do all kinds of promises and forced me to take oaths' Jai replied.

'Of not meeting her and conversing to her?' I asked.

'Yes, similar stuff. I've felt like my guts burning since then. Mummy is not trying to understand me' he said.

In between the conversation, I forgot to tell you about Ankita. She's been Jai's first and last crush. He has liked her for ages but now she doesn't reside in the town. So they speak sometimes on the phone but the frequency has kept on decreasing lately. As far as the limit goes, once Jai paid two hundred bucks to a boy for a napkin that Ankita left on her desk. How big an idiot he is? He could have spent the money on us. This is what I am acquainted with about her and now you know as much. But I know just a bit more; I've seen her photos and boy, isn't she cute? Just the right kind of girl for our amusing Jai. Now, back to the discussion.

'I can comprehend what would be going through aunty's mind, isn't there someone who could make her realize about your true camaraderie with Ankita?' said Vicky.

'Yeah, my cousin knows all about it and understands the situation pretty well, I guess. But she dares not discussing it with mummy. At the end of the day, the fact remains that Ankita is getting away from me' said Jai.

You would be thinking where on earth does this type of tuition take place? The boys are going on and on and there is no stopping them. But I told you already: we study with full concentration and full fun. This is how we live life. Whether it's the right way or not, I've no idea. Meanwhile, sir was telling us something about the crystalline structure of solids. I won't go into much detail since this book is not meant for competitive exams aspirants.

As the time ticked by, I realized that life was not going to be any easier in XII. This was the first chapter in chemistry and I felt my ass being blown off already. Let the scientists do the business, why should we dent our pure and nonchalant brains?

'So what do I do now?' Jai asked as we left the coaching that day. We were all together as Karan was to give us a treat, I don't know why. Whether any matter or not, Karan was the one to give us a post-tuition party every alternate day. Sometimes Shubham and myself also spent something but only when occasions beckoned.

'I dunno' said Shubham, 'never experienced anything like this in my entire life. Honestly, I've never had a true girlfriend. Anyways, it's not the time to go into my out-of-resources life and think something about Jai. You two have any suggestions?' he asked gesturing to Karan and me.

'No notions, man. Haven't got a clue. As far as my agenda says, it would be better not to get in touch with Ankita for some time and try to win your mother's confidence. When everything looks settled, try talking to aunty and explain the circumstances' said Karan.

'That's good. Deserves a consideration, right?' asked Jai.

'Yeah, could be pondered upon' I said pushing open the strikingly crafted door of Heera Sweets. This was our place, small and noiseless. It offered us good food, with reasonable charges. Vicky, Ravi and others studied physics at the same tuition as well. However, we four who are enjoying the delicacy right now studied the subject elsewhere.

'Okay, final. This is the step I'm going to incorporate' said Jai as he ordered samosas for the four of us.

Karan was fast, he really was. Two bites and the samosas swirled in his stomach. As soon as he completed his mini-meal, he asked for four bottles of coke from Sharma ji. We knew each staff of this shop; after all we were taking evening meals here for a year now.

'Bye then, see yaa tomorrow' said Karan and waved. He and Jai were off to one direction and Shubham and me to the other.

'Bye' Shubham and I said in unison.

I was tired by the time I reached home. I was studying a chapter in physics in my room when my sister dropped in. Candidly, she was the one whom I trusted for all my problems. I told her about Jai's trouble and the solution that Karan had put forward. She pretty much agreed to that and told me to dress up as we had to go out for a wedding in a club.

'What the hell? I'm already feeling sleepy and now to go out for a wedding, really sucks' I said.

'You can't do much to change it, can you?' didi asked.

'No, I can't but at least I can try and persuade papa to come back sooner' I said and forwarded myself to my closet to change.

The party was all the same. The same menu, same people, same atmosphere and the entire *sames* one could think of. However, going out to a boring night wedding served me a purpose. I found a girl of my previous school who was looking exceedingly sensuous in her skirt and red tops. I didn't talk to her much in the school but here I had nothing else to do. So, I dropped in.

'Hi Shikha, you here?' I said as I reached her with my ice-cream melting at the rate of three liters per hour.

'Hi Arjun, great to see you' she said calmly as if we had been talking for hours.

'This is my father's cousin's marriage ceremony. So I had to come, what about you?'

I was left stupefied as my question had backfired. I had no idea at all whose marriage was taking place and what relation did I have with the bride. Oh good, at least I knew I was from the bride's side.

'Dunno, though I guess I'm from the bride's side' I replied blankly.

'What? You don't know whose marriage is taking place?' she further asked with an expression as if I had not answered *in which country would you find the Taj Mahal?*

'No, I don't and that's not a big deal. I have no interest in family backgrounds and I came here for a bit of change from the hectic schedule, that's all' I said justifying my presence.

'Oh, all the boys are the same' she said in a low voice but loud enough for me to hear. I wondered who the other boys I was being compared to were.

'Nevertheless, where are you presently?' I asked to change the topic.

'In Notre Dame. My word, my parents are searching me. I'll have to leave. Give me your cell number' she said and gave me a pen and her hand to scribble the number on her palm.

I held her hand tightly for more than only writing the number. It felt smooth and I wondered which soap she used for hand-washing. I wrote the number in big bold digits: 9124128124. She wrote her number on my palm and rushed away to her parents waving her hands towards me.

At least I made some use of coming here, I thought as I sat on the rear seat of the car for the return journey back home.

That night I slept with dreams of Shikha with me on a date in a five-star hotel. It wasn't the first time I had such kind of dreams. The only new-fangled thing was that the girl had changed from Juhi to Rubi to Shikha. I guess this type of thoughts keep coming to you in your sleep because you don't have it in real life. You need something to keep yourself energetic and motivated to reach your goal and here lies the power of God. At least he keeps you in high spirits in your dreams so that you don't wander away from the original track. Good night!

# 4

# Search for Einstein

I feel you all are by now aware of the fact that I didn't study physics where I studied chemistry. I along with my three friends studied the subject there previously but gradually we came to know that the teacher was not up to our standards. By saying this, I don't intend you to make out that our standard was high; it was below par. So I had to get hold of a new physics teacher for the four of us who could begin from the grass root level.

I didn't have a great idea about the educators in the town and hence I thought it would be better seeking advice from papa. He was at home when I came back from the school on Wednesday. At lunch, I referred about the matter. As for the permission for staying at Pranav's place, I had plenty of time to ask. So, I didn't bring that topic in between the channel of communication.

'It's mid April and we still haven't caught up with a physics teacher' I said picking up the chana dal kept on the other side of the table.

'Yeah. It's getting late, isn't it?' papa asked.

'Of course it is. You don't know anyone who could help?' I quizzed.

'Hmmm... let me think...' he pondered and I could see twitches on his forehead.

'What about Dilip uncle?' didi interrupted.

'Most certainly. He could be worth it and I can ask him if you would like to' papa said gesturing to me.

'Yes. You told me he was a good teacher when I passed Boards, but we ignored him that time around. He could be useful and he teaches somewhere nearby' I said.

'How many of you are there?' papa asked.

'Four of us. Jai, Karan, Shubham and me' I replied at once.

'Okay, give me the number' said papa and didi sprang into action. She is just so obedient, I thought. And again as I said, it was didi who solved all my little complications.

She gave Dilip uncle's cell number to papa and he dialed it and talked for about two minutes. I think papa was told to send me along with my friends to uncle's teaching place in the evening. And I'll tell you what; I was dead right.

'I talked to him and he sounded excited at the prospect of getting a few more students in his batch' papa said as soon as he ended the call. 'Go with your friends to Tapasya Complex in Boring Road at six in the evening. He teaches Monday alternate and he would tell you about the timing there.'

'Perfect, that settles it then. I'll call all my friends and tell them to reach here by five so that we could be there at the precise time. Hopefully we get it all right' I said as I completed the splendid lunch.

I went and called the four of them and everyone was happy that finally we had got hold of some teacher who was not necessarily Einstein but could end our long-awaited woes.

'Alright, I'll be there sharp at five' said Shubham over the telephone.

'I hope our search ends here' I said.

'Surely will. You know anything about the fees?' he asked.

'No, not yet. We would be told about that there. But what I do know is that it's Monday alternate' I answered.

'Suits us fabulously well, see yaa at five then' he said.

'Bye' I said and concluded the call.

I wasn't feeling sleepy today like the other days and so I thought it would be a good idea to tune into the TV. The news channels were all the same blowing there heads off on the return of the Indian cricket team from the Caribbean after they were knocked out of the World Cup by the hands of our neighbours Bangladesh.

The media in our nation works like this: they just want to earn dollars by flashing insignificant hearsay and don't focus on information that could be of some importance to the common man. They feel it's better to telecast Ash-Abhishek marriage ceremony live than to broadcast the inhuman survival conditions of the Indian farmers. I turned on to the movie channels to find if they had something interesting to deliver and they had.

One of the channels was premiering *Rang de Basanti.* I had seen the film before and it did leave me influenced. My notions matched the director's, I thought. Exactly how this country lives was portrayed brilliantly with rocking music. By the time the movie drew to a close, I felt asleep.

****

'Wake up. Jai is waiting for you' said didi in a one hundred twenty decibel sound to arise me from a horrendous dream that showed me being thrown out of the school by the principal himself since I had kissed a gorgeous girl in between the assembly. The principal and the teachers didn't enjoy my act of bravery; though the students applauded my performance wholeheartedly. Realizing the zero probability of the dream in real life, I woke up.

'Jai is here so early, he is so unpunctual' I said in a drowsy voice as the clock showed half past four.

'It's better he is early rather than being late' commented didi.

'Yeah, you are right' I said as I moved towards the refrigerator for water. A sip of cold water was all I needed to break my haziness.

'You were sleeping?' asked Jai as I reached my room. I noticed he was reading a parchment that held the stamp of SKOAR.

'Yes, I was. I am not being able to fill the quota of my day's sleep since the school timings have changed' I replied.

'That's not the case with me; my school is great at timings. Though I've to admit, you must be facing problems. Nonetheless, what is this?' he asked showing me the parchment.

'Oh, that. That was an invitation letter sent by the SKOAR magazine to attend a Gaming Expo. You know SKOAR, right?' I asked.

'Yep, I do. The only Indian magazine dedicated totally to video games' he said and began reading out the letter.

## SKOAR! 2007
## India's Biggest Gaming Expo

### Invitation to participate and volunteer at SKOAR! 2007

*Dear Arjun,*

*As you well know, right from its first issue in February 2003, SKOAR! has established itself as the premier computer gaming magazine in the Indian subcontinent. Our aim is to spread awareness about video games and how they extend to beyond being mere "entertainment". Our last Expo held at Bangalore was a major success, which drew over 50,000 visitors across all age groups. Our aim was to let the visitor know first-hand what the "gaming experience" is all about.*

*With the stupendous success of the first two iterations, SKOAR!'s gaming expos have firmly established themselves as the premier gaming event in the Indian subcontinent. We now look forward to SKOAR! 2007, to be held at New Delhi, to set even higher standards of public participation and awareness about the unique experience that gaming has to offer.*

*As a regular reader of the magazine and an active member of the Indian gaming community, I would like to invite you to be a part of this experience and see for yourselves how computer games can open the doors to a whole new world of* ***interactive entertainment.*** *Entry to the expo is absolutely free, and people across all age groups are encouraged to experience the next big thing in youth culture.*

*I look forward to seeing you at SKOAR! 2007. The details of the venue and date are attached overleaf.*

*Yours Truly,*
*Badri Narayan*
*Editor, SKOAR! Magazine*

'You have huge amount of interest in video games' said Jai as he folded the letter and kept it inside the envelope.

'They are a great source of *interactive entertainment* as you might have just known by the epistle' I said.

By ten past five, Karan and Shubham had joined us too. I served them the *nimbu paani* mummy had just prepared.

'Shankar sir would take a test on Solids on Sunday, how am I supposed to prepare?' asked Karan.

'Dunno, we won't be able to persuade him to take the test later this time around' I said.

'No, we won't. He is very adamant on taking periodic tests on the completion of every chapter' Shubham said.

'We'll see how to deal with that later. As for now, let's get a move on. Einstein might be waiting for us' I said and gestured them to proceed to the door.

'How are we supposed to go? Karan, have you brought your bike?' asked Shubham.

Karan signaled no by moving his bald head sideways. He had shaved off his head recently as someone old in his village had passed away. Also as I said you, Karan was a massive dude and he could have easily laden the four of us on his Bajaj Avenger. Once he had done that when we were returning after watching a movie in the Assoc Multiplex. And the fact that we didn't have to go anywhere far, it was a good option but now no more as he had come using the public transport of the town.

'I'll get the car, it's free at the moment' I said and I could comprehend by the expression on their faces that they were pleased.

'Drive carefully' said mummy and gave me the keys.

'Don't bother, mother' I said as I turned the ignition on.

We were about one kilometer away from our destination when the car suddenly jerked and stopped.

'What happened?' said Jai with terror making his face look like a deer running away from a lion.

'Dunno...' I said and then realized what mistake I had made. 'Oh, you know what? I had put the car in the first gear instead of the third' I said and started it again. Some onlookers stood nearby to find more about the problem.

'That made the car shudder?' asked Shubham.

'Yes. I assume when you are driving at sixty and suddenly you put the car into the first gear, it jerks and stops' I said.

Within five minutes of this incident, I found myself parking the car near Tapasya Complex. On a white board that hung from the building was written in black letters:

**DILIP KUMAR,**
**PHYSICS TEACHER**
**FIRST FLOOR,**
**TAPASYA COMPLEX**

'Good, he is at the first floor; we won't have to ascend a lot of stairs' said Jai as we moved towards the flight of steps. 'How would he teach? *Na munna na, tumhe apni maa ki saugandh ki tum kal mechanics padh ke aayoge'* he continued impersonating our great bollywood legend. He was a master at it; could have surely tried himself in the laughter shows flooding the TV screens.

'Now, be quiet' I said as we reached the door which led to the coaching center. It was half shut; the optimists would say it was half open. I knocked on the gate thrice and realized I hit the timber hard enough as my fingers hurt.

'Come in' said a loud voice from inside and we entered. There sat Dilip uncle on a comfortable chair. The room was diminutive and could barely accommodate a wooden table and five chairs on one of which sat the owner. I had met Dilip uncle two or three times before and thus faced no problems recognizing him.

'So, how are you, Arjun? It seems that you have lost a lot of weight in a year and a half' he said and I wondered how accurate he was about the time when we had last met. You would have certainly noticed one thing about me by now; I wondered a lot. When you have nothing else to do, it isn't a bad alternative.

'Oh, have I? Going to the school by my bicycle is responsible for it' I said with a genuine smile as the four of us seated ourselves on the remaining chairs.

'You four want to study physics here?' he asked.

'Yes. All of us studied in the same coaching previously but began facing problems lately and so we had to leave' explained Shubham.

'What kind of problems?' uncle inquired.

'The teacher dealt with only *numericals* and didn't focus much on the base. Thus, we felt our concept was not on the level it needed to be' I said.

'No problems, I feel you won't face anything like that here and even if you do, you are free to interrupt' uncle said. It's high time; now I need to replace *uncle* by *sir*.

'When will we have to commence, then?' Karan spoke for the first time making his huge company being felt.

'Day after tomorrow. I teach four days a week including Sundays. The timing for Monday alternate is three to four thirty and eleven thirty to one on Sundays. Any query?' sir questioned.

'We reach home at two thirty after school. So it would be tough for us to be here at three. Can timings be changed?' I asked.

'No ways. You'll have to be here latest by quarter past three. I can't change it or other students will have to suffer' he spoke calmly.

That wasn't the best solution to my problem. Yet, I had to compromise as I had no other option.

'And what about the fees?' asked Jai.

'Don't worry about that now. First study for a week and then we'll talk, okay?' sir said and I was glad at the prospect of experiencing *demo classes* for a week and then discuss about monetary matters.

'Okay. Then shall we leave?' I asked for sir's consent and he nodded.

'Thank you, sir' all of us said together and stood up and ensued towards the door.

'Great. The meeting was short and to the point, the man seemed cooperative. He is?' asked Jai gesturing to me.

'Dunno... I haven't met him many times. So, no comments though I feel your surveillance might be correct' I replied as I took the driver's seat.

Shubham had to go out with his father and thus he left us as soon as we reached home. Karan and Jai stayed for a while and the latter talked about bringing the former's plan to action.

'Let's see if it works. I'll be trying beyond my limit to win mummy's confidence. It's not as uncomplicated as one thinks it to be. You have to pretend hard to be *mama's boy*, you understand?' said Jai as he steered his *Porsche Boxter* right down the terrain in his all-time favourite game.

'Steady, Jai, or you'll break Arjun's keyboard' said Karan and it was then that I noticed Jai was pressing the buttons as if he was Fernando Alonso (since Michael Schumacher had retired by the time I wrote this book and so I didn't employ his name) and my keyboard was his car's steering wheel.

Also, you must appreciate how much my friends cared for me, whether on the cost of pinching other's boots was entirely their choice.

'Fuck you' said Jai as he finished last in the game even after making use of the *break-the-keyboard* tactics. 'Here I'm discussing how to get on with life and you are concerned about the bloody typewriter... err keyboard.'

The effect of the mistake Jai made near the completion of his sentence was that the seriousness of the situation diluted. And it was for good as I didn't want Jai to get grave and all messed up again. He is much better when he is in a blissful frame of mind.

'You'll succeed, Jai and it is only possible when you are hopeful of it. So, man... drop the solemnity now and be yourself' I said pleading him to be the Jai we all loved and cherished.

'You are right, time to talk about other things' he said with a smile on his face which authorized that the guy was ready to get a move on.

*****

And as the remaining two of my friends left, I mused about a matter. Jai called the keyboard *bloody* and I hate him for that. If it wasn't for this brilliant creation of man which we call the keyboard, I wouldn't have been able to complete even a page of this tome. Whether it deserved a completion, as I've already said, my dear readers, rests on your shoulders.

Mummy served me my favourite dinner that night and it was enough to put me into a decent night's sleep. These are the things with hunger and sleep; you need to get one of them right for the other to follow. As usual, I dreamt of the most beautiful things on the planet. I'm not going to tell you much about them as this manuscript is about my life and valued friends and not about me wandering in the biggest fantasies of the world.

Get the ball rolling, folks!

Tomorrow is a new day!

# 5

# New Day, New Pickings

Yes, this is another day of my pointless life. I've certain ambitions but I'm far from the track which leads to those. As a high school student, one is expected to get right in the groove to yield better results for the future but I surely don't consider me being a part of that *one*. But you know I can't afford to be a naysayer all the time. So, I've decided to find the positives within me.

Maybe God has created me for something else. By *something else*, I intend things which are out of the reach of common man. Everyone wants to become big but only a few of them do. It's not everyday that a Bill Gates or a Sachin Tendulkar is born. I don't want you to infer that I dream of becoming that big but most certainly I want to fulfill the minimum parameter that confirms that a man is *successful*.

This is all I know about me and I'm communicating it to you. Even if you are being bored, you have to tolerate as I'm the narrator and you are experiencing the events from my eyes. Okay, enough of my third-grade philosophy...

Let's get back to the *tale that is being told by an idiot, full of sound and fury, signifying nothing*

(Shakespearean people will understand the idiom better).

As I was taking the customary morning coffee, didi came up and sat near me grabbing the newspapers. You would think what's special in this? There is. She usually has her college after nine and so she rarely wakes up this early. I sensed something particular in her eyes. And forgive me, but why do you always expect anything special... after all this is a common description of common people.

'You know who is coming here today?' didi asked with excitement clearly visible in her eyes.

As a matter of fact, I didn't know who was coming but just to see the aggravation on her face, I replied otherwise. Boys love irritating their sisters without a cause and vice-versa.

'Yep, I do. Papa told me yesterday only' I said.

'How could have he? Uncle called after you went to bed' she said with a gloomy look on her face now as I had robbed her of the break-a-new-news satisfaction she gets every time after delivering anything fresh. Also, as you might have just noted, it was some uncle who was approaching. Now I had to only guess who he was.

'Don't worry; I don't know anything about it. Tell me who is coming?' I asked stopping to toy with her emotions.

'You liar', she said with the prospect of telling the information again making her appear joyful. 'Kumar uncle. Yes, it is him who called and he is coming today for a week long-stay here.'

'Oh, great' I said standing up and moving towards the kitchen for sugar as the coffee had less of that.

Kumar uncle was probably papa's closest friend along with JP uncle who resided in Delhi. The three of them were *true* friends as we call it and they were famous in the university as the *trio*. It is from these three friends that I've understood the meaning of amity and its overwhelming powers.

Though now they all resided in different towns, whenever they got together, there chemistry was worth making a movie on. J P uncle wasn't coming but even the thought of two old friends meeting after quite some time put me in the best of my spirits.

'Is he coming with some purpose?' I asked as I returned to the table.

'No, nothing in particular, as far as I guess. Just to meet papa and relive some past memories but isn't that a purpose of its own?' didi questioned.

'Of course it is. It is a greater purpose than any other' I replied finishing the morning quota of my twenty-one-hundred-calories-a-day consumption.

******

The school today was much of the same until the third period when Pranav discussed with me some elementary matters that make a guy's life interesting. As usual, we were sitting on the last bench and the teacher didn't seem of much use who was giving a dreary lecture on *Computer Applications*. So we thought it was better chatting.

'Liked someone in the class?' Pranav asked as he skimmed through the novel Zayed always brought to school for passing time. I, at once like most of the other chaps, understood what he anticipated.

'Yeah, I have. You see the one sitting on the right side of the third bench on the column adjacent to ours'? She is nice, isn't she?' I asked.

'Yes, she is. You know her name?' he quizzed.

'No, I don't but...' I was replying when Rajiv interrupted.

'Surbhi is her name. You should refer to me for problems like these' he said and turned to face the blackboard.

Rajiv was a master at it. He could give you an entire bio-data of any girl you pick in the class. Whether it was Neha or Farah, Julie or Jasmine, he knew every girl from top to bottom. Don't take it literally, man... What I want to say is that if you want to know the background of anyone of these young women, he is the dude to approach. Anyways, back to the all-important dialogue.

'Oh, good then. Surbhi is the one I fancy' I said with a broad beam on my face.

'Fine choice, Arjun' said Pranav and gave me a tiny hug. 'And I fancy someone as well, someone else though' he added with a smirk on his face sharpening his already-sharp features.

'Who's that?' I asked with anxiety clearly audible in my voice. What's there to be so excited, I thought, and couldn't come up with the answer.

'The girl sitting on the last bench of the corner row' he said and I raised my head to get a better look. Damn, lovely she was and Pranav's selection had made my job easier of choosing between her and Surbhi. Yes, I fancied her as well but now no more. I don't obstruct the way of my friends unless it's extremely important.

'You know her name or should I consult Rajiv?' I asked.

'Shalini' he said in a highly humble voice and this time Rajiv didn't enrich our minds with his superior knowledge. 'She was previously in Zayed's section and I've liked her from my first day in this school.'

'Oh, age-old love,' I said, 'have you ever talked to her?'

'Nope, didn't get the opportunity, you see,' he responded, 'I'm always so busy.'

'Yes, of course. You have some hundred appointments a day breathing down your neck. How do you manage, Prime Minister Sir?' I joked.

'DJ' Pranav said.

It's not the DJ you might be thinking. It is the abbreviation for a *dardnak joke*. I know I'm not a good joke-maker but these friends are a lot worse. What would have gone wrong if Pranav had appreciated my mood-setting effort and not categorized it as a DJ? But then, these are why they are friends, right? They tell the truth regardless of its consequences.

We told all our mates about the new selections Pranav and I had made. And the time of this famous announcement as you would have presumed, was the recess.

'Surbhi????' Shubham asked with surprise filling his voice.

'Why? You know her?' I interrogated.

'Idiot, I was in her section for whole of the last year and I'll tell you what, she was my first crush at this place' Shubham said.

'First crush... was she?' Raj asked.

'Yep, but I never talked to her, you understand? I spent the entire year just appreciating her flawless beauty' Shubham answered.

*Flawless,* it must be said, was too much a word for her. Yes, she was beautiful but wasn't Miss Universe or something. These days, however, I don't find even them strikingly beautiful. Maybe my beauty-judgment parameter has increased its level to new standards...

'I hope that isn't the case with you, Arjun' said Kishore stamping his presence.

'It won't,' I said, 'I'll remain hopeful and up for the challenge.'

'You're right. It's a tough challenge' commented Shubham, 'she is quite a decent girl and I haven't seen her talking to many boys. Remains with her friends most of the time and doesn't even laugh at the nonsense jokes.'

'Oh, brilliant analysis,' Pranav said 'you have done a great job in the last year. Tell me, however, what do you mean by *quite decent*?'

'Fuck you, that's just using words' Shubham said.

'You've any idea about Shalini?' Pranav consulted gesturing to Shubham.

'No idea, man. I'm not Rajiv who as you all are seeing, is yet again busy observing girls' replied Shubham.

Absolutely, Shubham wasn't Rajiv. And it was true, Rajiv was twenty meters away from us noticing the girls who had come up to the washroom for rinsing hands.

This was his favourite lunch break's *break*.

Everyone streamed in our section to have a look at the girls we had chosen for spending the year and they all were more than content with our *choices*. Ravi, however, was a bit more excited.

'Go, go talk to Surbhi' he insisted as I asked Vicky for his bottle of water. This was the case, someone brought food, someone brought water, and I brought nothing except me.

'Have you gone nuts?' I said, 'it's not an ask-for-a-book situation, my dear Shahrukh, it's about creating a positive impression on her at the very first meeting. So, let me get a good idea and then I would proceed.'

'And when will the idea strike?' he asked.

'Anytime, as a matter of fact. Those come with pre-vibrations in your mind; it's got to be natural' I said.

'What are you two talking about?' Kishore said as he joined the two of us.

'Nothing, I told him to get a move on but this dull dude hasn't got the pluck to drop in' Ravi summarized.

'Goodness me, I told you the idea strikes from inside…' I was saying when Kishore interrupted.

'You are talking about Surbhi and stuff?' he asked.

'Yes' Ravi and I said together nodding our heads.

'Oh, what the hell! Haven't you got anything else to talk about other than girls and sports?' he said.

Yes, sports… I haven't talked about sports that much but a quarter of my life was dedicated to it. I can't live without it and can't wonder the world to exist sans it, either.

From soccer to squash, from Federer to Ferrari, I loved everything related to sports. Sensation arises from competence, competence arises from rivalry, and rivalry arises from you-know-what. May it be an India-Pakistan cricket match, or an Arsenal-Manchester United football contest, they all get the planet rocking to their tunes. Anyways, back to the dialogue….

'Ravi, get out of here, someone is coming' Vicky said in a terrified voice as I saw Varun Sir coming in.

You know what? Ravi was screwed. We forgot to keep track of the time in our discussion. Entering a section that doesn't belong to you is prohibited in this school, and adding to that, being found in another section when a teacher arrives is quite a punishable offence. Don't go nuts; this is the way this place works or otherwise why would we have detested it…

Adding to the seriousness of the situation was the fact that Varun Sir (I don't know if he deserves to be called a *sir*) shared a bitter relationship with Ravi since his time in the school and so he was always searching for a reason to screw him up.

'What are you doing here? You are in section C, I suppose?' sir asked as soon as he saw his age-old foe.

'I had... I had come to take the English book' Ravi replied with extreme anxiety making his voice sound desperate.

'And where is the book?' the teacher said in a calm voice.

'Oh... sorry... I had come to return the book.'

We called him Shahrukh but goodness me, he was a total contrast. Acting was not his part of cake; rather he was rubbish at it. Further, his dreadful delivery had put him in more trouble.

'Okay, no problems. Come with me to the Vice-Principal, he would help you' sir said with an expression of a carnivore animal that gets hold of its prey. Most certainly, here Ravi was the prey.

The educator returned within five minutes with a mission-accomplished look on his watermelon-shaped face.

'He got a letter, he'll have to be here in three days with his parents or else he would be suspended' the teacher announced to the class with a sense of pride adding to the loudness of his voice.

During that period, I thought of the consequences of the mistake Ravi had committed but instead came up with the cause. After all, I was the one who involved him into the conversation and thus the situation arose.

'Nothing would happen. I've got about eight or nine letters so far and it's not a worry at all' said one of the high *letter-receivers* of our class.

'Don't they do anything if the parents don't come?' I asked as I was not much experienced in this field.

'No, not a bit. Actually, all this letter-thing is just a formality, you understand? Just to show that this place takes heed of what the students are doing. They forget the name of the students they give the letter to the very next day. So there is nothing to be concerned about' the boy summed up the state of affairs.

Oh, good. There is not much to worry, I thought and got back to what I did best all the time in the school-gossiping about topics from hell to heaven.

It was the last period of the day when Pranav reminded me of the football match we had to play in the weekend.

'I talked to everyone. All the guys are ready. I think we'll have enough boys for a full-fledged match to take place,' he said, 'you asked Rebu?'

'Not yet but I'll tell him by tomorrow. Let's see who wins this time' I said.

'We'll prevail this time, just gotta see that we don't give away goals easily,' he said, 'and what about the stay at my home?'

'Haven't talked about it, either, maybe tomorrow, there's still time' I said.

'Not much, though.'

We met Ravi after dispersal and the fact that he had been handed a letter by the school authority didn't seem to bother him too much. At the end of the day, he was rather happy that it served him some purpose.

'All the students in your class would have known me; see, I got famous' he announced proudly as we boarded the bus. I returned home by the school-bus these days since I had to come here by the bicycle from next week onwards. There's a bus-pass for students who use school transportation services but they don't check passes for about a fortnight at the start of a new session. So here lied a chance for students like us to consume at least something which this *boring place* had to offer.

*******

The coaching went roughly the same way, not to mention the ragging that Karan took of a new boy who had come to take admission and was pretty much scared seeing the former's huge structure.

'Sing *Aashiq Banaya Aapne* using your nose or else we'll make you do push-ups' said Karan.

'What is this? You take ragging in tuitions?' the boy asked.

'Who's the boss? We are... so just do what you are being instructed to...' Karan was saying when Jai interrupted.

'I've an idea. Why not let him go and propose *nurse?*' he said.

Karan was ecstatic hearing the notion. Wondering about *nurse?* She's the only girl at our coaching. She studies chemistry here and is preparing for Medical Colleges Entrance Examinations, I feel. Why we call her *nurse* can be answered employing Vicky's logic; he says the girl isn't great at studies and so wouldn't go as far as becoming a doctor, so *nurse*.

I know we've no rights to decide about her future but this is just making fun and further, the girl doesn't know about her fancy-name one bit, thus no worries. Getting back to the ragging session, I must admit I enjoyed it. The boy had no options left, so he took the obvious way but we had to guarantee him that we'll take care if the girl reacted otherwise. But I was sure she won't. Also, just to remind you, our teacher had not yet arrived.

'Hi', he said with a smile, 'I'm new at this place and...... I love you.'

'What? Are you crazy? I've met you for the first time' she said with a dismantled look on her face.

'Oh, these boys forced me to say that' the boy said gesturing towards us and we burst out laughing. I could see a smile on the girl's face as well and so I knew everything was fine.

'Sorry, Esha, just having some fun. Hope you haven't taken it seriously' Karan said to the girl and yes, her name was Esha.

'No problems... it's fine' she said and turned towards the door as we heard footsteps. It was our teacher who had just arrived. And then he taught about all those stuff that according to me is of least use in practical life. *Will you tell me how can drawing a 3×3 matrix can help an engineer build a bridge?* If you know the answer, you deserve to be in the IIT.

I think here is where our country has not made full use of its available resources. In spite of producing the brightest minds of the world continuously over ages, our motherland has not yet reached the supreme heights that it ought to. After all, it is the Indians who have helped America and other developed nations grow their economy like hell.

My dear boys and girls, it would be better serving your nation for less money rather than living in America like a third-grade citizen. I'll tell you something- the feeling you would have earning enormous amount of money is nothing compared to what you will experience when you would do something that might help our country prosper. It's not that I'm getting patriotic; it's just an Indian youth expressing his desires.

******

When I returned home, I found Kumar uncle already there. I was pleased to see him and so was he. I guess we were meeting after quite some time.

Just as I bent to touch his feet which according to our mythological books is the most courteous way to show your regards to elders, he said, 'You are a grown up boy now, Arjun' and hugged me. Good, now I was gradually moving towards what they call the *adult* group.

'So uncle, how are you?' I asked.

'Very fine by your wishes' he said and parked himself on the chair he was sitting when I had come.

'How are your studies going? Preparing well for the competitive exams?' he questioned.

'Quite fine', I said, 'I'm getting screwed'. I muttered the latter part so that he couldn't hear.

'What? What did you say?'

'Quite fine, uncle' I said.

'That's what I expected from you,' he said, 'by the way I heard your school is closed tomorrow, right?'

'Yep.'

'But why?'

'Dunno, our school is hosting some state-level exam, so gotta be shut' I said.

'You are free tomorrow, then?' he asked.

'Of course,' I said, 'you got some work for me?'

'No, I just think it would be a good idea to take you out for lunch' he said.

'It's isn't good, it's great, you have made a nice start to your stay here, sir' I commented.

'Anyways, I've to go to the market now, got to see how much the city has changed' he said.

'I'll come as well' I said pleased at the prospect of going out on a relatively cool night. Also, I had just returned from the chemistry tuition and I didn't want the subject to occupy my already preoccupied mind. Hence, a change was surely needed.

******

Just as I was wandering in the *Aditya* shopping complex while uncle was busy observing a bookstore, I felt someone hitting me hard on my back. I thought of retaliating even vigorously but when I turned, I changed my mind. It was Shikha to my extreme delight.

'Hi,' she said, 'our second meeting in three days. What's up?'

'Hi, just came along with uncle, he had to buy some books' I said trying not to sound too excited. Oh, I forgot to tell you what she was wearing. A pink salwar suit was making her look dazzling again. She wasn't as good a year ago, I thought.

'Tomorrow is my birthday,' she said, 'so bro has come to buy a present.'

'Nice. Where is he?' I asked.

'There' she gestured to a boy who I at once recognized as Shikha's brother. I had never seen him before but the two of them had strikingly similar features. He was at a distant corner appearing full of activity. It was even better; I had got more time to talk.

'Tomorrow there is a small party at home,' she continued, 'some old friends are coming. Will you come?'

I was left gaping and I couldn't help myself change my expression. It was a total shocker of a question. How a girl whom I rarely talked in the previous school could invite me on her birthday and that too after a year of our separation? I was unsure about what to answer.

'How-how can I? I mean I don't even know your friends' I replied.

'No, you know most of them and even if you don't, I know you,' she said, 'it'll be like a small get-together.'

'But I'm engaged tomorrow' I said.

'At what time?'

'In the afternoon, I suppose.'

'No worries, the party is in the evening at about seven. You are coming now, surely?' she said.

'I might feel a little subdued, after all not many people other than you would know me' I said.

'That's no big deal, I told you already' she almost growled.

'Okay, I'll try.'

'It's not about trying. You'll have to be there' she said.

'Alright.'

'Good. I'll remind you once so that you don't forget' she said as I saw her brother approaching us.

'Meet Rohan, he is my brother,' she introduced, 'and Rohan, meet Arjun, my friend.'

'Hi, Arjun' he said.

'Hi' I replied with an extensive smile. 'Gotta go, uncle is waiting, nice to see yaa both.'

'Bye' the brother and sister said in unison and I was off.

Returning home, I recalled the whole day. It was quite big, to say the least. And it was mostly full of girl characters ranging from Surbhi to Esha to Shikha. I also considered what gift would be appropriate for Shikha. I wasn't able to reach at a decision, so I thought it would be better consulting didi. I left that work for the next day as I was tired by my overloaded itinerary.

It might be a tiring day tomorrow as well but I'm quite prepared for a *sweet* hectic day.

Be positive, think positive, live positive, dudes...

Let's see what beckons...

# 6

# Fabulous Friday

'Eeeeezzzzzzzzz.........' the alarm went off so loud that I almost fell from my bed. Yeah, I know school is closed today but the alarm doesn't. You know it's automatic and all that stuff... so it rings every day at the same time until you change the settings. I surely forget these things and thus get my sleep broken every now and then. What's more disappointing is I get barred from my astounding dreams...

Now since I had woken up this early, I thought it would be better to take a morning walk around the colony lane. Mummy was the only one other than me in full consciousness, so I told her that I'm getting out for a small saunter.

'Don't go very far' said mummy as I put on my new branded shoes. My elder sister had gifted me those on my birthday which was a month ago.

'I won't,' I said, 'and stop behaving as if I'm a two-year child going out to fight a battle.'

'These are the problems with your young-generation mentality. Even a three-word guidance seems to be a serious comment' muttered mummy.

No, I think mummy was wrong. Oh! Not about the advice... about the fact that it contained three words. It involved four and that too when you consider *don't* as a single word. It could be substituted by *do not*.

The sun was not in its full stride and so my stroll was quite comfortable. I saw a throng of people with anxiety marking their faces as I launched myself on the main road. On getting closer, I realized that a biker had clashed with a kid and the latter was damaged with blood sprouting from his legs like a fountain. Would you believe who the biker was? It was Ravi.

I could see Ravi ten meters away from the occurrence of the accident surrounded by three very angry-looking men.

'What the hell? Was it you who ran into the kid?' I asked in a low voice as I approached him. Ravi looked relieved on seeing me but I wondered if I could help him in a situation like this.

'Who are you?' a man with white locks and a pumpkin-large face asked me.

'Oh, I'm his friend' I replied gesturing towards Ravi.

'You know what, Arjun? It wasn't entirely my fault. I tried to control the motorcycle but the kid came in front of it in a split second' stammered Ravi.

'See, these guys are so irresponsible,' said another man who seemed to be the strongest of all. 'He has hit a toddler right now and says it isn't his fault.'

'I didn't say that,' Ravi reacted, 'I just said that it wasn't *entirely* my fault.'

'Oh, good. Now you are even arguing' said the strongest man.

'Leave it,' I said to Ravi.

'Okay, sorry. What do you want me to do?' my friend asked the three men.

'This sorry will not do' the third man answered speaking for the first time, 'you will have to come with us to the police-station.'

'W-w-what?' I and Ravi retorted simultaneously.

'Yes, absolutely. I suppose a police case is charged if one rides irresponsibly' said the white-haired man calmly.

The complacency in the man's voice made Ravi look grimmer. His expression embodied a feel that said he was searching for ways to get out of the mess he had just created.

'Sir, we're students and as my friend is saying, it was not entirely his fault. Of course he could have rode better but you know it was unintentional-'

'-I had tried my best to save the kid but it was out of my hand. We can't survive all this police stuff, please let us go' Ravi completed the sentence for me.

'We can't but there is a way out' the brawny man said.

'What?' asked my dear friend with desperation clearly making his voice sound like *Lata Mangeshkar's.*

'Give the victim's family some money and get out of here.'

'But the victim's family isn't here. They've just taken the kid somewhere, maybe to the doctor' Ravi said.

'Then give it to us. We'll transfer that to them' said the less-speaking guy.

Oh, this is the beauty... In our nation, you can get yourself out of any problem if you've one thing in your possession-MONEY. Yes, this five-letter word is probably the solution for most of your difficulties. You have the currency, you are the boss but if you don't, god is the boss.

'How much do you want?' I asked.

'We don't *want* the money; instead we are saving your friend's ass. So speak properly' said one of them.

'Sorry, but what do you expect from us?' my comrade questioned.

'At least five hundred bucks.'

'Ohhh! But I don't have that much' said Ravi.

'Then come to the police.'

You see, this is proper blackmailing. Every second common man in the town knows this way of earning funds. They are all far from the pain the kid is experiencing, but will get the bottle of whisky they want to satisfy their bellies.

'Sir, please try and understand our position' I pleaded.

'Okay, four hundred, nothing less than that' said the pumpkin-faced man.

'You have some money?' Ravi garbled to me.

I was sure I had none but just checked my pockets for the friend's sake. Unbelievably, I had a hundred-rupee note.

'Yep, I've hundred' I said.

'Okay, I've twice as much', he said. 'Sir, we have only got three hundred rupees, nothing more. Please accept this and let us go.'

'Alright. But don't ever ride like this or else you'll land into more trouble. Get out of here' said one of the three men extending his palm so that Ravi could give him the money.

Bargaining works here as well. Even in a situation like this where you are being asked for cash to help the victim you have just hit...

'Thanks' said Ravi, and we rushed away from the spot as quickly as we could.

'Where the hell were you going by your bike at this time?' I shrugged showing him the watch on my wrist.

'Aunty told me to bring a packet of milk,' he said, 'the vehicle was free, and so I took it.'

Yes, Ravi lived with his aunt and uncle. Previously he didn't reside in this town and had only come here last year for higher studies. He wasn't rightfully serving his purpose though...

'And you rode like this?' I said as Ravi took the turn towards my home. Right now he was precautionary and steady.

'I told you the kid came out of thin air.'

'Okay, I understand. I faced problems like these when I was learning to drive the car. Though I must say I haven't yet hit anyone as hard' I said.

'Fuck you. I know how to operate a motorcycle, you idiot, this can happen with anyone. What a friend you are?' he protested. He parked the bike so hard in front of my house that I felt that he met another accident.

In a couple of seconds I realized that he had...

'Whaaaam' the bike screeched as I fell down quite dramatically. My dear friend was still on the vehicle as he tried hard to control it. He was able to do it finally in another two seconds.

It was a small fall and thus I hadn't got hurt. Ravi's anger had just spilled its beans.

'Relax man,' I said as I got up back on my legs. 'What on earth has happened to you?'

'Proving to you that I know how to ride' he said and was off the next moment. This man had gone nuts. I hope he reaches his home safely...

******

A great day lay ahead for me. I was so busy today... I had to go out for lunch with uncle, I had my first day of my physics tuition today, and I had to attend Shikha's birthday party...

So let's start with the first part of my fabulous Friday-the Lunch.

'I love this place, it's just so cool' I said as we entered *Soda Fountain* which according to me was the best among all the restaurants in the city. Though it might sound modern by its name, it was amazingly traditional in its approach. The food was excellent here and so were the costs, perfectly reasonable.

Oh, I forgot. The word *we* here includes uncle, didi and myself. Papa had to go out for some work and mummy didn't enjoy having food anywhere other than home, so only we three.

'The restaurant has changed so much' uncle said as the gatekeeper opened the door for us. You guessed it right. Apart from being traditional, this place was antique as well. It has been in the city for more than sixty years now.

'You bet it has. They change the interiors every now and then, they're crazy' didi commented.

'They are *not* crazy; it is the fact that they focus so much on every small thing that keeps this hotel full every time' I said pointing to the overloaded tables all around the semicircular hall.

By the way, we got a table near the far-end of the entrance. Good, the air-conditioning system was just above.

'You both decide about the food,' uncle said, 'but I'll decide about the soup.'

'Sure' I said as I handed him the menu.

'Tomato sweet and corn would be fine; it was such a specialty in our times.'

'It still is, I believe' didi said gesturing to me to tell whether she was right.

'Of course it is great as ever before,' I said, 'our choices match, uncle.'

Honestly, the soup was remarkable and so was the food. Chicken dishes were excellent and I enjoyed them the most; both uncle and didi are vegetarians.

'Delicious, how do they do this?' I asked as I broke the fluffy leg piece into several parts.

'That doesn't matter, you are not going to start a restaurant' didi said.

'But I love this. If somehow I knew the recipe, I would have tried it every alternate day' I said.

'Don't shit. I doubt that you would have seen the kitchen even once for a month' didi shrugged as she quietly broke her *paneer* piece into two.

'Whatever,' uncle joined, 'the foodstuff is still exceptional.'

My stomach was *four-third* full by the time I finished my plate. Yes, I had eaten more than my day's quota.

'Which ice-cream do you prefer?' uncle asked.

'Chocolate' both didi and I said at once. My whole family loves the flavour other than mummy; she likes vanilla.

Even if the chicken was up to my neck, I couldn't afford to miss the ice-cream. The desserts here were even better. The conclusion you might have arrived at would be that this place was heaven for food-lovers; right from start to end, it had finesse to offer.

'Lovely' I said as I licked the remaining square inch of my sweet dish, 'it's incredible.'

'Thanks for the treat, uncle,' didi said, 'but tell me is there any slight reason for this?'

'No, just wanted to have some time out with you kids, isn't that enough?' uncle asked.

'More than enough' I answered as I saw the waiter approach us with the bill.

******

We returned home soon enough as I had to go to the physics tuition at three. At quarter to three, the phone rang.

'Arjun, you at home?' Karan's voice said from the other side as I picked up my mobile.

'Yep, but where are you?' I asked, 'you told you would be here at half past two.'

'I'm not far off, calling from a telephone booth.'

'Alright, come fast, I don't want to be late for the classes on the very first day' I said. As a matter of fact, I was a regular latecomer. I tried hard but could not change my habit of unpunctuality. But seriously man, first day of new coaching- I wanted to be there before time.

Within a few minutes, Karan was at my home but no one else was-neither Shubham nor Jai.

'Where is Jai?' Karan asked as the clock on my wall showed the small needle strike three.

'And where is Shubham?' I added.

'Oh, I forgot. Shubham called me and said that he had been out for some work. So he would join us at the coaching directly' Karan said.

'You told him to remain downstairs if he arrived first' I said.

'Yeah, I did. But where the hell is Jai?'

'How am I supposed to know that?'

'You aren't. Okay, tell me- what excuse would Jai give when he arrives here late?' Karan said.

'Dunno… that's a good question though, could be tried for IIT. However, I think he would say that he wasn't getting an auto' I said

'I believe that he would say that he caught up with some friend on the way here' Karan put forward his valuable thoughts.

You can draw positives out from everything. Though I am not the biggest idealist, I know what's the better part here- Karan asked about the excuse Jai would give for being late when he arrives…

At least Karan thought that Jai would reach here. I got a sense that he would have forgotten that we had tuition today, he would be sleeping at this time with dreams of Ankita hovering in his cerebrum… Well, I don't know what that is-but I'm sure that's a part of our brains; I read about them in previous classes. However, whether it has anything to do with our *dreams-functioning*, I don't have a clue.

'Ting-ting' the bell rang and I ran up to the door at once hoping that it would be our very dear laggard. Indeed it was.

'Sorry' said Jai, 'I believe I'm a bit late?'

'A bit, what the hell? You see the time; it's almost half past three' said Karan joining me to see the visitor.

'What is this, Jai? You promised you would be here very early' I added.

'Sorry man. I am not late intentionally. The auto suffered a puncture and it took time repairing it.'

Great, an absolutely new justification…

At least I was close; I'll tell you how- the excuse had something to do with an auto.

'C'mon, get a move on now. Shubham would be waiting' I reminded.

Within ten minutes Shubham was also there with us guessing the reason for our untimely arrival.

'You guys suck. First day and we are forty minutes behind schedule, don't you all care?' said a furious Shubham. I only saw him in such mood when he was asked to give his opinion on our school.

'We do, only this boy doesn't' said Karan signaling towards Jai.

'Okay, enough, let's enter' I interrupted.

Today we didn't go inside that tiny room. Instead we entered another door which was adjacent to the first. A very lean looking man was present there reading the day's newspaper. He must be the assistant, I thought.

'You four are the new students?' he said looking at us.

'Yes.'

'Why are you all so late?'

'Due to school' Shubham said. It was good we blamed the *boring place* for our misfortunes. After all, it deserved that, maybe even more; it had bestowed us with so many disappointments in the last one year.

The door to the class was about five meters away and it was closed. There were glasses separating the assistant's table from the classroom, so we could see what was going on inside and so could the teacher. Dilip Sir gestured us to come in.

One thing amazed me and I bet it amazed my friends even more; there were about twenty five students inside the room and you know what- only three of them were boys.

'Are there no boys here?' I asked the assistant.

'There are three of them and now seven, I believe' he answered.

'Fantastic, it rules. We don't have many of our friends here but we do have girls' whispered Karan as we opened the door for entering into the room where the teaching was in progress.

'Yes, it's incredible, I'm happy to say the least' I added as we took the last bench. There were two columns of desks with boys only occupying the last rows of both the columns.

The educator was teaching something related to electrostatics but I wasn't able to understand as we had joined the chapter in between. We were relaxed however as the teacher had said we need not worry as he would make up for our absence later.

'Don't worry, you've missed the starting of this chapter and so you may face problems. I'll teach you all that later but you just try and concentrate to get even the slightest in your grasp' said Dilip Sir coming close to us as the rest of the class was busy solving a question he had given on board.

'Okay?' he asked seeing our anxious faces. We nodded.

'Meet me after the class is over today' he said and moved towards the front rows to check what the other students were doing.

'There are so many of them here, it would be difficult for us to *choose*' spoke Shubham softly. Most certainly, *them* here refers to the girls present at the place.

'Yeah, but I can't see any of their faces from here' I said as we were sitting on the last bench as you already know.

'The one in pink seems good but the final decision would only be made after I see her features' added Karan.

'Right. But she is looking sexy' I commented.

'Exactly, that's the word, she's *sexy*' said Karan.

After the class was over, we waited to see the girls' faces. The sexy one was not only sensuous, she was gorgeous as well.

'What a combination,' I said, 'not only she's good-looking, she has an excellent figure.'

'Leave her for me' shrugged Karan.

'No ways, I'll look after her' I said.

'What a friend you are?'

'There are so many of them here, you choose anyone else' I gave him an alternative.

It was so easy- you choose a girl and everyone else will start calling the girl yours. Whether you talk to her even once doesn't matter at all. No other guy in your circle will want the girl for himself. That's friendship. So, as told, now the girl belonged to me. She was Arjun's girl as they call her.

'Okay, sacrificed her for you' Karan said in a grim voice as if he had given me his age-old home.

'Let's go and meet sir if you two have finished your *girl-distribution process'* Jai said.

'Yeah, enough choices, we'll talk about that later. First get down to the important work; finalizing our stay here' added Shubham.

We went to the same tiny room we had met sir day before yesterday. There were two girls discussing some matter with him.

'Sir, the exam was fine but I made some silly mistakes,' said one of them, 'I hope that doesn't hamper my entrance into a good medical college.'

'No, it won't. You'll get through, be a believer, not a loser' said sir. He was quite positive in his approach and I started sensing my time here would be good in the coming days.

'The mains of AIIMS are still left, just go through my notes thoroughly and I assure you that it'll help' he added.

'Alright, we'll try our best', promised the other girl. 'Should we leave?'

'Yes, sure and best of luck for you upcoming exam' sir said.

By this time, all four of us had already occupied the seats. As the girls left, sir turned to us: 'You have come in between, so some problems might exist but I'll take care of that. In the next class, we'll start with a new chapter and then you can totally concentrate from there on, okay?'

'Of course, sir.'

'One thing needs to be made very clear,' sir said, 'you can't be allowed here so late.' I knew this was coming; we were forty minutes late on the very first day. 'It's better to come individually and early than to arrive late in a group. This way you can also tell your mates what has been taught before his arrival if he is late. You understand?'

'Yes sir, we'll try to be punctual' I said.

I was happy our teacher didn't make a mess out of it. Usually, people will tell you much more than this; I mean they will torture you for forty minutes if you are forty minutes late. If you understand what I'm saying, it's great and even if you aren't, it's great all the same; that'll not affect your idea of comprehending the plot.

'Also tell me, you liked the environment, I mean the atmosphere is good for studies, right?' demanded sir.

I didn't understand what he meant by this. However, we liked the *atmosphere,* maybe for other reasons but liked it nonetheless. You can't have an aversion to a place filled with so many girls around you.

'Yes sir, the place is superb, superb for studies' Karan said.

'Good, I expected that from you,' sir said, 'meet you all in the next class, then?'

'Yes sir' we said and moved towards the door. He was always so much to the point, didn't waste time discussing rubbish issues.

'Karan, take out the money, we'll eat ice-cream' said Jai seeing an ice-cream parlour in front as we came out of the coaching.

'Mate, I've no money, you can check my pockets if you wish' Karan said.

As soon as the words were out from speaker's mouth, Jai approached Karan's pockets.

'Alright, come, let's eat' said the big friend of mine pushing Jai's hands away.

'I'll give half the money' said Shubham making relief mark Karan's face.

'What'll you all take?' the shopkeeper asked as he was giving out the flavours the customers demanded.

'Mango.'

'Chocolate for me.'

'Butterscotch here.'

'Vanilla' I said in spite of chocolate being my favourite flavour as all of you might be already aware of. But I couldn't have it two times a day.

I think I should have replaced the name of this chapter from *Fabulous Friday* to *Ice-cream Day* as I was having my second ice-cream of the day and most probably would have one more at Shikha's place. Oh boy, I forgot one thing- I hadn't yet wished Shikha on her birthday.

As soon as this thought came to my mind, I took out my cell phone and started to call Shikha. Yes, most certainly I had saved her number on my mobile.

I was successful on my first attempt. What are you thinking? I'm talking about getting the connection right on my very first try. These private mobile connection companies are rarely good at this- you have to try a hundred times to make a call. However, they are superb at one thing- SUCKING MONEY FROM A COMMON MIDDLE-CLASS INDIAN.

'Whom are you calling?' asked Shubham.

'Shi-'

'-Hello...' the sweet voice of Shikha spoke from the other side.

'Shikha there?' I said.

'Yes.'

'Hi, Arjun here. Happy birthday, Shikha.'

'Thanks, so nice to receive a call from you, I thought you would have forgotten.'

'No, I've a bad memory but not that bad' I said.

'Do you know my address?'

'Nope, I haven't ever been to your home.'

'It's simple. 234, Saket Villa, Airport Road' she said.

'Yeah, it's easy. Are you sure it'll not be awkward for me to come?' I inquired.

'Not at all, how many times will I tell? Be here by seven.'

'Okay, I'll be there' I said.

'You have to and don't forget to bring a gift she said followed by mirth making her voice sound even sweeter.

'I won't.'

'Bye, see yaa' she said.

'Bye' I said and ended our small but yet vital conversation.

'Who was she?' asked Jai as soon as I kept the cell in my pocket.

'A girl of the previous school' I answered calmly.

'You never mentioned her to us, did he?' Jai said gesturing to other mates.

'Nope, he never did' Karan said.

'I met her only three days ago and haven't talked to her much, was just about to tell you all' I said.

'What? You said she is a girl of your previous school and now you say she met you only three days ago?' Jai said.

'Fuck you. It means I met her after a year' I said.

'And you are going to her birthday?' asked Shubham, surprised.

'Yeah, but how do you know?' I backfired.

'Fool, just now you said on the phone' Shubham said.

'Oh, I'm developing a tendency of forgetting things nowadays', I said. 'Okay, let me explain,' I continued seeing amused looks on all of my three friends' faces, 'her name is Shikha. She was in my previous school and I hadn't met her for a year until I ran into her in a marriage ceremony on Tuesday. She met me again yesterday and asked me to attend a small party she's giving on her birthday, that is, today, and some old pals are also coming. Fine?'

I hadn't spoken breathlessly that long for ages. I hope the matter was quite clear now and I soon discovered that my buddies understood the situation well.

'Great.'

'Keep going dude.'

'Why don't I ever discover a girl of my previous school?' said Karan gloomily.

'That's sheer luck and boy, isn't Arjun lucky?' said Jai.

'No man, we are just friends' I clarified.

'We're also your friends but you don't ever talk to us like that over the telephone' protested Jai.

'Oh man, you all are too much' I said.

'Are we? I think that applies to you' Shubham said.

'How is she?' Karan interrupted.

'And what do you mean by that?' I asked.

'Idiot, what else can he ask? He means how does she look?' Jai detailed the question.

'Quite good,' I said, 'I'll tell you the truth- I didn't find her good enough when I studied with her but now she has drastically changed.'

'Yeah, you start to value things only when you lose them' Shubham put forward his philosophy.

'No guys, she has really changed, in fact she has developed' I said.

'Developed?' all three of my friends said at once, amused.

'Yeah, she was like a cute child a year ago but now she's a girl, an absolutely lovely girl' I said.

'You've started to like her or what?' said Karan.

'Dunno, though I guess I find myself cheered up in her company.'

'Oh, that always happens with you, you are happy in every girl's company' Jai commented.

Yes, Jai was right. I found myself very happy in the companionship of girls- the only condition was that the ladies must be beautiful, or *my type* to be precise.

So whether it was Surbhi, Shikha or the *Sexy Waali* (the girl I just now chose for me at the Physics coaching), I would've enjoyed their camaraderie anytime.

'Whatever, enjoy the birthday' Shubham said.

'Yes, that's the priority, the prime business of life is to enjoy' Jai said.

'I surely will' I assured them.

'You bought the gift?' Karan asked.

'No, I forgot that as well' I said.

'What have you thought of giving her?'

'No idea, I thought I would ask didi, she might give a good suggestion.'

'She certainly will,' said Jai, 'by the way, let's get going, Karan, I've to go out with papa as well.' Jai and Karan resided in the same locality and so they usually went back together.

'Bye, meet yaa tomorrow' said Karan and opened the door of the shop to move out. I didn't realize when the money to our desserts was paid; I guess I was too busy thinking about Shikha's birthday present.

As soon as I was home, I approached didi. I hadn't yet told her that I had to attend a party tonight, so she was just a bit taken aback at hearing I had met a new girl of my previous school who had invited me on her birthday.

'The girl you met in the wedding ceremony,' she recalled, 'you said you met her after a year.'

'Right.'

Everyone was surprised; and I had to clear their doubts every single time.

'So you are going?'

'Yep, I am.'

'What the hell-'

'-I'll explain the matter later, just tell me what an appropriate gift would be?'

'What does she like?' didi asked.

'Oh, very good question, if I would have known that I needn't ask you' I said.

'She was your classmate, you ought to know something about her, and I mean maybe a bit about her likes and dislikes.'

'No idea, none at all, I told you I didn't talk to her much.'

'And all of a sudden she has become your very dear *friend*?'

'What's there in attending a birthday party?' I asked.

'No problems and I didn't say anything about that' didi said.

'So tell me, what should I buy?' I questioned.

'What's your budget like?' didi said.

'Not much, maybe a hundred and fifty bucks, I can't afford to spend much with David's birthday also approaching.'

Now, surely, you must be thinking who on earth is David? He is just another one of my friends. I knew him through Pranav and he is a damn good guy. Quite overweight, he is extremely polite in his behaviour. The best part of his friendship is; no wait, if David would read this? Leave it, even if he does, I'll still say: so as I was saying the best part of his friendship is that he has a shop of DVDs and so we get any new movies right from there. You know what; his father doesn't know that he gives DVDs to us.

'When is David's birthday?' didi asked.

'On Tuesday.'

'Not very far' didi said.

'Oh god, will you please tell me about the gift' I beseeched.

Seeing my pleading face, didi finally had some mercy on me. Thank God, now I'll get the answer.

'A cute teddy bear will do, girls love those kind of stuff' didi said.

'Hmmmm... fine idea, I think' I said pondering hard.

'That would be reasonable, even affordable' didi added.

'Right,' I said making up my mind, 'will you come with me to the shop?'

'Oh, you can't even do that much?'

'I can but you know better' I said.

'Okay.'

Once you get yourself inside a gift shop, you can't help yourself from exploring every item and so was the case with me. I wanted to buy everything; from watches to showcases, from photo frames to CDs but I guess I had come to buy a simple and cheap teddy bear.

'This is lovely,' didi said spotting a small yet cute teddy bear, 'the brownish pink colour is so soothing.'

'Yeah, it's fine, I'll buy it' I said.

'You don't want to check around more?'

'Noah, I don't think I can restrain myself from buying everything I see.'

'Sure?'

'Yes.'

'Okay, also give her a card, prefect combination' didi suggested.

I didn't know how much the gifts would cost but was pretty certain that my pocket would allow it. However, my expectations never meet reality and so it was this time as well.

'How much?' I asked as I saw the shopkeeper gift-wrapping the present.

'Two hundred.'

'What, is that teddy bear so cost-'

'-It is, Arjun. These shops demand this much' didi said in a low voice.

'But I told you I can only spend one-fifty at the maximum' I said trying to keep my decibel-level near to the ground as well.

'No problems, I'll contribute, after all your friend is my friend' didi said raising her eyebrows.

'Thanks, you are so good' I shrugged touching her cheeks.

'Okay, okay, no need for your *maska*' she said.

One thing is good with these shops- even though they ask for more than required in terms of money, they will make up for that by doing other things. For example, the gift was so pleasantly wrapped that I forgot the two hundred bucks its contents cost me and my very cute sister. It also made me remember the present Pranav had given to Zeesha. I hope you remember that also.

'What time will you leave at?' didi asked as we were on the way back home.

'She has called at seven. So I'll leave at quarter to seven' I replied.

'Have you gone nuts?'

'Why?'

'You want to be there at the precise time?'

'Yes, why not? We should be punctual' I said

'What the hell? You are not punctual for your school and coaching and want to be punctual for a mini-birthday party?' didi retaliated.

'But what's bad about it?'

'There's nothing bad. It's just stupid. There'll no one there when you reach, no one except Shikha's family' didi said. At least now she had started to address Shikha by her name rather than *the girl of your previous school.*

'Should I be a little late, then?'

'Surely. You should be there by quarter to eight, maybe at eight if you ask me' didi proposed.

'Okay tell me- how will that help?'

'This will make her realize that you are quite busy and have taken out precious time from your schedule to attend her birthday' didi said.

'That does sound nice' I said.

'It only doesn't sound nice, it's *actually* nice.'

'Alright, I'll reach there at about eight or a little before' I said.

'Good.'

# 7

# Shikha's Birthday

As recommended by didi, I left my home at half past seven in the evening. I had survived many temptations of reaching at the party at time but then the thought of the importance I might receive at going late came to me, and so I stuck with the *unpunctuality rule.*

The Airport Road is probably one of the most posh localities of our city. I had no problems finding out Shikha's home; it was a three-storey multicolour building with big black gates marking the front. A distinctly big lawn sprawled in the background though I couldn't get the best view of it as the sun had set. On one the gates was beautifully written:

**234,**
**Saket Villa,**
**Airport Road**

I opened the gigantic black gates and soon realized the lawn was cleverly developed. There were about eight trees marking the turf's boundary and also lights were present at every corner. Two of them were lit up which was enough for me to find the call bell which stuck itself out on the front door.

I checked out the time before ringing the bell and it read 7:48. Okay, the time is perfect and so is the setting; ring the bell.

A woman in her early forties opened the door who wore a hugely embroidered saree making herself look like the Maharani of Rajasthan. Nevertheless, I guessed she would be my friend's mother.

'*Namaste* Aunty,' I said, 'I'm Shikha's friend.'

'*Namaste beta,* come in.'

I couldn't see Shikha or any of the other guys whom I had expected here. The hall was quite big decorated magnificently with balloons and ribbons. A lovely chocolate cake laid in the middle of the room enough for my complete weekly diet of the flavour.

'Shikha and her friends are upstairs, go and join them' aunty said signaling to the staircase on the right side of the foyer.

'Thanks' I said and ascended.

'Shikha, your friend has come' aunty said in a loud enough voice for the birthday girl to come out of her room and see the visitor for herself.

'C'mon Arjun,' Shikha said gesturing me to approach her, 'why are you so late?'

'Sorry, coaching and stuff' I said putting my feet on the final stair.

'No problems, at least you have come' she said and held my hand taking me inside her living room.

Oh, I recognized the guys at once, and even the girls.

'Hi, Arjun, what's up?' said Rishabh giving me a high five. He was my classmate a year ago and I hadn't seen him since.

'Hi, I'm good, what about you all?' I asked a common question.

'Rocking, dude' said Raghav who too was my classmate previously. Now listen, everyone here was there with me in my previous school and so I won't give each of their introductions. 'Will you present the gift to Shikha or take it home with you?'

Oh, the gift was still in my hand and I think I forgot to present it to Shikha probably because I couldn't take my eyes off her brilliant face which glowed today like a gem. Moreover, she looked soothingly stunning in her dress.

'Happy birthday' I said as I forwarded the present towards Shikha.

'Thanks' she said accepting it with a beam that illustrated her emotions. Am I getting a bit *poetic*? Forget it, all I want to say is she looked strikingly spectacular today, tonight rather.

There were seven people in the room which included Shikha and me. Three of them were boys whom you are already aware of and the girls consisted of Rakhi, Richa and Esha. Yes, the Esha who studies at my coaching, the very same...

'Esha, you here?' I asked, surprised.

'Why, you know her?' Shikha asked.

'Yeah, I believe we study at the same coaching' I replied.

'I'm Shikha's cousin' said Esha clarifying my doubt.

'Great, that's cool, now I don't have to introduce her and you know the rest of them, right?' said Shikha.

'Most certainly' I said though I didn't use to talk much to any of the girls at school, after all I didn't talk much to even the birthday girl earlier.

It was now only that I noticed that the living room was even more decorated than the hall downstairs. There were amazingly shaped balloons covering much of the room with a big HAPPY BIRTHDAY banner right on the wall adjacent to the TV.

'Beautiful decoration dude, seems cool,' I said unable to resist my temptations to praise the craftwork, 'had you brought an interior decorator for this job?'

'Esha and I have done it' said Shikha proudly.

'Oh, Esha is not only a future doctor; she is also a future decorator' I said with a half-smile. It was only ironical that I used the word doctor for her; usually nurse sprang to my mind at once on seeing Esha. We had been calling her from that name for a year now and she didn't know it. This was my assumption but hell, how wrong could I be.

'Why do you all call me *nurse*?' asked Esha in an intensely calm voice as I seated myself near her. She said it in a low voice as well so that only I could hear.

'What-?'

'I know it.'

'We don't-'

'Now c'mon, I am aware with the title you all have given me' she said.

I didn't know what to utter next. I was totally shocked and more than being surprised, I was embarrassed.

'We just joke' I said blankly.

'Not a very good one, I'm hurt' she said.

'What are you two talking about, tell us as well' said Shikha patting Esha on her back.

'Just discussing about the tuitions' I said finding no better answer.

In fact, I was glad that Shikha had interrupted us as I had nothing to say to Esha that might have cheered her up.

'Forget about studies for the moment at least' said Richa for the first time since my arrival.

'Yes, let's get the boots rolling, thumbs up for some music?' Shikha said.

'Absolutely, let's rock' said Raghav.

Shikha proceeded to the music system which was placed beside the TV. She brought a paper kept on the table and handed it to me.

'What's this?' I asked.

'Collection of all the songs I have,' she said, 'choose whichever you want.'

'How about *Khalbali?*' I asked to everyone. There is something about A R Rahman's music that keeps all us teenagers going. There is not a friend of mine who doesn't adore him. So, as expected, everyone agreed.

One more thing is interesting here. Since I share everything with you I'm going to tell you this as well-while writing this extract I was listening to the very same song (as I wrote this entire piece on my *lovely* computer).

Shikha switched off the tube lights and powered some flickering bulbs on. I think this kind of lighting was done in the room just to give a feel of a discotheque and boy, didn't it provide just that.

Some people including Esha were quite shy to come out and dance in full stride, so we had to just drag them on. I persuaded Esha so that I could somehow bring her into a better mood.

'Great man, it's fantastic' said a totally *bouncing like a rubber ball* Rishabh; he was all over the place. And his way of bopping was surely a mixture of every dance from salsa to samba, from tango to bhangra.

*'Khalbali hai Khalbali....'*

The songs kept changing and so did our dance steps. Finally, I thought of creating something productive and switched off the music system.

'Whattttt-'

'What happened?'

'Why did you switch it off?' asked quite a furious Rakhi. So now girls were enjoying the party more than the boys.

'Dear Lady, can I have the royal pleasure of dancing with you?' I asked to Shikha stretching my right hand and bowing down on my knees. I had measured every word I had spoken and it did work out well enough.

'Sure, I'll love to' said Shikha taking my palm into hers. This was it; I felt I had done something big.

And Raghav whistled giving the situation an even better outlook. I had set up the mood, man. The music was again on in its full flow.

'You dance like a professional' I said tightening my hold on Shikha's waist ten minutes into our ballet. Up to this point, neither I nor my partner had said a word; we were just involved in seeing each other's eyes.

I wonder I'm getting a bit romantic. Thank god, at least I have dared to...

I looked around to see what the others were doing. Everyone was as engrossed as I was- Raghav had found Richa and Rishabh was dancing with Rakhi. Esha was nowhere to be seen but I had no time to care about that now.

'Yes, I've done a bit of dancing classes' replied Shikha coming even closer. I could feel her breathing on my cheeks, I could feel her locks tangled to mine, once I even felt her lips on top of mine-all this was getting so charming, so charismatic, so captivating. This was the first semi-kiss of my life; in fact it was even lesser. Nevertheless I would remember this for the rest of my days on earth...

I did not know how quickly the time was passing- I had forgotten it was getting late, I forgot about going back home, I forgot about everything other than me and Shikha drowned into each other.

'Guys, enough fun, let's get down, aunty is calling you for cutting the cake' said Esha who had just now joined us back.

The cake was delicious, simply exotic. I ate a couple of large pieces, one which Shikha stuffed into my mouth and the other which aunty gave me. I met uncle and other people in the family including Rohan whom I already knew.

'What are you plans for the future?' asked Shikha's father who was sitting beside me during the dinner. The food was as good as the cake and by now I was sure the dessert will follow the pursuit. I don't know why but uncle gave me a kind of a *father-in-law* tinge. I know this is funny but it is true and I can't keep you away from the better things of my life.

'I want to do MBA from a reputed institution,' I said, 'maybe from somewhere like an IIM.'

'And what about IIT?'

'To be frank to you, uncle, I must say that I'm not hugely attracted to the IIT. It's just that I'm following the trend.'

'What trend?'

'I mean people say engineering plus management is better, so just for the sake of it, you understand what I'm saying?' I asked.

'Yeah, I'm. Just be yourself and you'll succeed. Life isn't easy but it isn't tough either' uncle said.

'Right.'

'Right uncle, just what I'm trying to explain to him' said Rishabh who was listening to us so far and thus dropped in his thoughts.

I looked at the time while having my last ice-cream of the day and it showed half past ten. Unbelievable, I had not yet received a call from home; maybe didi had explained it to papa and mummy.

Esha was sitting on a chair five meters away and I joined her so that I could help myself away from embarrassment.

'Are you still thinking about that?' I asked.

'About what? Oh, about *nurse*. Forget it, it's over' she said and this certainly increased my level of confidence. After all she was taking it lightly.

'You know, we didn't want to hurt you, we keep funny names for friends as well, you know I'm called *Mougli* by pals' I lied justifying the cause.

'Yeah, I understand, your name is very good though' she said with a smirk.

'Have you really forgiven me?' I said.

'What's there to forgive? You are a friend and that's why I told you, otherwise I wouldn't have. And after all, it's not just you who calls me by that name.'

'Sorry again.'

'Now c'mon, that's more than enough, you are forgiven' she said.

'Thanks.'

'No thanks and sorry in friendship' she added.

'Cool, that makes me feel better' I was saying when Shikha interrupted.

'Thanks for coming, Arjun. This is for you' she said handing me a small teddy bear. It just looked like the miniature version of the gift I had given her.

'Oh, have you seen my gift?' I asked.

'Your gift? No, but why?' Shikha said.

'Just like that, you'll know about that later. By the way, why have you given me this?'

'Just like that. Consider it as a return gift.'

'Thanks' I said.

'No thanks in friendship' Shikha said.

'All you girls are the same' I said and burst out laughing along with Esha. Shikha, surely, didn't understand with puzzlement visible in her tired yet refreshing face.

The party was a nice one, I thought, as I proceeded to the exit of Shikha's home with other friends. I was near the door when Shikha stopped me.

'When are we meeting next?' she said in a low voice.

'You suggest?'

'Tomorrow?'

'Time?' I asked.

'Evening.'

'I've tuitions.'

'Okay then, on Sunday?'

'Sure.'

'Thanks once again for coming' she said.

'Great party, bye.'

'Bye, good night.'

*****

It was quarter to eleven when I was preparing myself for a nice night's sleep when my phone rang. It was Pranav.

'Arjun, sorry to call you at this time but why was your cell switched off?' he asked.

'By mistake, actually I didn't know it' I said.

'Ready for tomorrow's match?' he said. Boy, I had forgotten all about the football match we had to play. I had not yet informed Rebu and it would be coarse to call him at this time, more so when he has a common phone.

'Yeah, ready' I said.

'Told Rebu?' he asked.

'Yes' I lied. I didn't want to suffer offensive language before sleeping.

'Good, many players are coming, I've informed everyone' he said proudly.

'Yeah, we'll win' I said.

'Surely.'

'See yaa tomorrow.'

'Bye, good night' Pranav said.

'Good night' I said and ended the call.

Today was a tiresome day as expected and it feels even more tiresome when you don't have enough time to doze. However, it was football which was more important to me than sleep and so I kept my merriment going. As far as informing Rebu was concerned, I'll call him tomorrow morning.

Will we win???

Wait and watch...

# 8

# The Football Fixture

Finally after all the work, here came the chance of some play. Yes, everything was work; from going out for lunch to the physics classes, from buying the present to chilling out at the party, it was only that I enjoyed most part of these kinds of works.

The match was planned to start at seven and so I had set up the alarm for six so that I could call up Rebu. He didn't live very far from my house and so there were no problems in him reaching my home in less time. Therefore, the first thing I did on waking up was dialing our star footballer's number.

'Hello' Rebu's father voice echoed over the line.

'Good morning uncle, Arjun here. Can I talk to Rebu?'

'Oh, hello Arjun, good morning, and how are you doing these days? You don't call very often nowadays?' uncle asked.

'Just involved a bit too much in school and tuitions, uncle.'

This was my standard answer to the questions fired on me by various people and to be honest, it was quite an appropriate one.

'Wait for a second, Rebu is coming' uncle said.

'Sure' I said and waited for Rebu to arrive on the phone.

'Hi Arjun,' Rebu said, 'what happened, calling this early?'

'We planned a football match today and I forgot to tell you about it. Can you come right now to my house?'

'Now?'

'Yes.'

'What time will it commence?'

'At about seven' I said.

'How many people are coming?' he asked.

'I think about twenty' I said but I doubted my expectations.

'Great, okay I'll be at your place in fifteen minutes, fine?'

'Good, see yaa.'

Rebu was one of the few of my previous school's friends whom I was in contact with and it was partly because we lived in the same colony. We quite regularly used to play these kinds of matches and thus Rebu knew all my friends I had found lately.

Just when I was getting up off my bed on the way to brush my teeth, the phone rang and it was Rebu.

'Hello Rebu, what's up?'

'Arjun, I forgot to mention one thing to you.'

'What?'

'Pushp has come to his aunt's home and so we can call him up as well. Should I?' asked Rebu.

'Yeah, sure.'

'Okay, I'm coming along with Pushp.'

'Right, see yaa.'

Pushp is our friend who lives in a very distant neighbourhood but sometimes comes to stay at his aunt's place which is nearby. All we friends were separated after our tenth exams. Pushp and Rebu joined the same school after Boards and so it was through Rebu that I still kept in contact with the former.

Mummy was surprised to see me up this early on a non-working day. Mummies are usually the ones who are the first to rise in the morning in a family, don't you agree? If you don't, you might not be living with your mother.

'Arjun, going out for playing or what?' she asked as I finally completed brushing my already shining teeth.

'Yeah. Good guess, right on the money' I said.

'Will you have something?' she said.

'No, I can't play with my stomach full.'

'I'm not going to get you *pratha sabji* anyways,' mummy said 'I was just wondering if you'll want to have some coffee. I've no problems if you don't want to.'

'Sure, coffee would be great.'

With the completion of my morning coffee ended my wait for Rebu and Pushp. I was just out of the washroom when they arrived.

'Good morning, sir' Pushp greeted.

'Good morning, ma'am,' I said, 'your height increases everyday by an inch or what?'

Pushp was the tallest among all of us. He was about five inches taller than us or maybe even more.

'Ha... every time I see him I feel embarrassment, I've to tilt my head upwards by thirty degrees to see his face' Rebu said out loud half-laughing.

'Come, let's sit for some time' I said.

'Anyone else who'll join us here?' Rebu said.

'Yeah, David would be coming.'

We reached Pranav's home at the precise time, neither late nor early. He and other friends had never met Pushp before and so I introduced them to each other.

'Move on now, it's seven already' said David when everyone expected to reach Pranav's home was there.

'Yeah, let's be quick,' Ravi said who was the last to join us, 'we should start the match early, it would get hot as the day progresses.'

'As if we didn't know that' Raj said.

On reaching the field I realized that we had actually many players to play a *real* game. Twenty of us were present including Shubham, Kishore, Mayank and some others. Most of them were school-mates.

Just as Rebu was the best player in our side, there was one player in the opposition who usually caused havocs in the defenses. I won't take his name or else he'll blush when he reads this. See what an optimistic approach I have- I felt he would read this.

By the way, if he does read, he is as precious as you all who have taken out such valuable time to see my life, if he doesn't he is just a player in the other side whom I've to stop from scoring goals.

'So everything's fine, we've divided the players, we'll take the cross-end side in the first-half' said Nikhil who assumed himself as the captain of the side we were playing against.

'No problems' said Rebu showing thumbs up to me. I gestured the same in return. 'Arjun, I'll start playing in the midfield, you and Pranav move up' he added.

'Right' I said and signaled Pranav to join me. The match commenced and the ball was in our half when Pranav said something important.

'You talked to your parents about staying?' he asked.

'Nope, today or tomorrow' I said.

'You've to ask today' my mate said as if ordering me to do it.

'Why, tomorrow is a bad day?'

'Papa and mummy are leaving tomorrow in the morning.'

'Wh-'

'Pick the ball Arjun' shouted Rebu as I saw the ball coming towards me. I'm not the greatest football player and when you aren't that and the ball pops up suddenly when you are talking about something else, you are not expected to do the business. So, invariably, I couldn't keep control of the ball and the defender latched on to it.

'What are you doing? Concentrate on the game' said a frustrated Shubham who too was in our side.

'Sorry' I apologized.

Again when Pranav and I got the time, we continued to talk in pieces. This time both of us were noting the movements of the football as well.

'What did you say? They are going tomorrow?' I asked.

'Yes, I'll tell you at half-time' he said running towards the ball.

The match seemed to be quite dull with me unable to put up even an average effort. Rebu was still exceptional with his tireless runs and some of the other guys in our team supported him. We were twenty minutes into the game when the heroics of the superstar of our opposition team paid off. He single-handedly beat six players and put the ball into the back of the net in style. Luckily, I wasn't included in the six defenders. We were 1-0 down... his solo effort not only deserved his team's plaudits but our clapping as well.

'Well done' I saw Rebu saying to the goal scorer.

'C'mon, get into the game' he urged to all of us and I think it was the goal which really motivated us to give more than what we could. We dominated the game for the next fifteen minutes and the half-time was close by when another of their players struck a goal. We were 2-0 down...

Oh, I had thought we had come to *win* this...

'We didn't play well' said Nitish who was an important member of our side as we were walking down to the temple beside the field which provided cold water for the travelers.

'Not at all,' said Rebu, 'at least for the starting half. We can still win it though.'

'What? You think we've got any chance? We are two goals behind' I reminded.

'So what? *Only* two goals' said Pushp marking his presence.

'Yeah. That's the spirit, have confidence in your abilities' said Rebu.

*In your abilities...* What a joke? Rebu could have faith on his aptitude but I couldn't... though just for the sake of my friend, I nodded.

'Play passing game,' he said, 'we can do it. You all believe in me?'

'Sure' all of our players said at once. We had more confidence on Rebu than our whole team combined.

Just as Rebu was explaining the team the second-half tactics, I got to talk to Pranav.

'They are leaving tomorrow?' I said.

'Yes.'

'How did the plan change?'

'Grandma said the puja was scheduled to take place on Thursday but now it's on Monday' Pranav informed.

'You told Raj?' I asked. Raj was not with us, he was hearing to the important lecture Rebu was giving.

'Yes, he said that aunty will allow him if mummy calls at his home and asks his mother for the stay' Pranav said.

'I'll get the permission anyways I think but I'll have to talk today', I said, 'Raj, come here.'

Raj joined us in the all-important conversation as well.

'What?' he asked approaching us.

'You are staying at his home, right?' I asked.

'Yes, aunty will just have to talk once to mummy' he replied.

'At what time will you come in the night?' I said.

'At eight or nine, but why are you asking? We don't have to stay today' he said.

'But we have to *stay tomorrow*' I reminded. 'And you'll be going to school directly from his home' I kept on banging in the questions.

'Oh, I didn't think about that, it would be a problem. Yes Pranav, how'll we manage in the morning?' Raj said.

'Why?' Pranav said.

'No problems, we've school from eight and we'll be setting the alarm for six so that we get enough time to reach our homes and get ready' I gave a solution.

'Most certainly, that would do' Raj said.

'C'mon, let's get going' said Nitish and proceeded towards the field. We, like sheep of the shepherd, followed.

'Let's begin' said Rebu and gestured the match to restart just as he had done in the first-half. Hopefully, the consequences wouldn't be the same.

India is the home of miracles. This nation has unsolved mysteries written all over it from paintings of the Ajanta Caves to the magnificence of Taj Mahal. Talk about how Hanuman held an entire mountain on one hand or about the dead body of a priest kept for seven hundred years in good condition in a church in Goa, everything sounds mind-baffling. So was the case with us; I don't how but our team started playing some wonderful football...

As known, Rebu was the center of all the action taking place on the pitch and the amazing part was that the other individuals in our team were also performing up to a certain level.

Though we didn't get a goal in the next twenty minutes, we knew it wouldn't be far-off. Our star player was also looking satisfied with the effort other guys were putting in.

Pushp received the ball from Rebu half-way through the second-half and I thought he wouldn't be able to do much with it as he was quite far from the post and there were about four defenders and a goalkeeper blocking his site. But, as usual, I was wrong again.

'Whaaaaaaaaaaaaaam' and the ball was inside the net. It struck the inside of the post and went in. As everyone else, Pushp himself was not able to believe what he had just done. He ran like a mad man would towards Rebu taking off his t-shirt. It did look quite indecent but who cares when you have just scored a goal...

Now, do you know why the act by Pushp was *indecent*? No, not because he looked bad with his t-shirt off, rather his figure was one to be proud of, I had always secretly desired of being a man with his shape and height, but because it doesn't look particularly good when you are present at a public-place.

'Okay, we're still a goal behind; we have to get one more' Pranav said making everyone realize about the next target we had to achieve.

'Exactly, c'mon, let's tear them off' said Rebu and I think it was his never-give-up attitude that motivated us to try and at least support him.

We did play some breathtaking football (*breathtaking* by our standards and boy, our standards are not very high) but still didn't get the one elusive goal separating us from our opposite team, but that didn't stop us from banging in the shots. We were five minutes from the end when Nitish ran with the ball alone and finished off in style. There are so many players here; you might be forgetting who belongs to which team. So just for the sake of you understanding the result of the game, Nitish was in our team.

Finally, we were level with almost no time left to play. Everyone was considering extra-time in the back of their minds but not one man... the captain of their team, Nikhil. At the very last moment, our defenses collapsed allowing the boy a one-on-one situation with our goalie. And yes, our goal-protector was comprehensively beaten. And yes, the match ended with the goal marking the importance of individual talent in our low-profile style of play.

We had lost the match and you know the score, right? No? What are you doing reading this book? We lost 3-2...

'No no no, what were you doing, you should have come forward' bellowed an absolutely fuming Rebu to our goalkeeper, 'I can't believe we've lost this.'

'Cool down man,' I said patting him on the back, 'we've just lost a *game*.'

'Just a game? And you are saying this?' he said waving his hand in air in total disbelief, 'you were the one who said we've to win this at any cost, weren't you?'

'Yeah, I was but we can't do much now' I reminded.

'That's a good excuse' said Rebu.

'C'mon, let's have some cold-drink' Raj said trying to absorb the heated debate going on.

'Yeah, sure' said Pushp and asked all of us to join. Surely neither I nor Rebu could afford to miss the chance of drinking a cola after such an exhaustive period of play. So, both of us proceeded with the other guys.

Our discussion on *why we lost the game* continued moving into the road-side vendor selling all types of drinks from cola to *lassi* (hard-drinks were not on his list though).

'We should not have conceded more than one' Rebu continued taking a heavy sip of his favourite *Sprite*.

'Right, and maybe we could've scored more' Pushp added intensifying my agitation.

'We *could* have, but we didn't,' I said, 'let's forget it.'

'I can't' Rebu said.

'But why?'

'I don't want losing especially in a football match,' he said, 'and I've got a feeling of rivalry against the *Nikhil* group.'

'Exactly, so have I' Pranav said.

'Oh, have you? Then we'll try and win next time' Raj said.

'That's the problem, we say we'll try but we don't, I saw our players not attempting to take the ball if once out of their grasp' Rebu commented.

'Whom are you talking about?' I wanted to know.

'No one in particular, everyone if you consider seriously, even me', our star footballer replied. 'You know what, they are better at this, at least they have a chemistry going about themselves.'

By this time, we had all finished our quota of colas. We combined to pay the seller.

'Okay, when is the next match?' Rebu asked.

'Not fixed, most probably in the next weekend,' Pranav said, 'we'll let you know.'

'Fine, see yaa later, I'm getting late. Pushp, you are coming with me?'

'Yeah, thanks for calling me, I enjoyed every bit of it' Pushp said bidding us goodbye along with Rebu. Everyone else had already left, so now only Pranav, Raj and I remained.

'Talk about it today' Pranav reminded.

'I'll have to, there is no other option' I said.

'And you ask aunty to call mummy, then only I'll get the nod' Raj jogged Pranav's memory.

'Absolutely, should I ask mummy to call at your home as well?' Pranav asked gesturing to me.

'No, I don't think that's needed, I'll let you know otherwise.'

'Okay then, I'm leaving, I'll need a shower after such a marathon match' Raj said and this was exactly what was on my mind. It seemed as if he had read my mind, after all that's why we're friends. No? Yes, you are right. Any normal person will need a bath after such high calorie-consuming bit of play.

'So am I, bye' I said signaling an auto to stop. David had already left, so I had to organize my own way of transportation for reaching home.

'Bye' said Pranav as Raj and I boarded the already overloaded auto. You'll have to agree on one thing with me. Public Transport System in India is ridiculous. Yes, I understand that we got independence late and all that but we could've still improved on all these little things that mark a country's growth, couldn't we? In some of the other big cities, the situation might be better but most certainly it wasn't such here.

There are so many things that I would like to change at this place and many others which I would like to eradicate, yet I love my nation. Maybe that's the reason why we call our homeland a great one.

Moving away from the topic of progress of our country, let's talk about the progress of my plan about the stay at Pranav's place. It would be so much fun staying with friends a bit more than we usually do but for that I had to get my parents' permission which I was sure I would get quite easily. However I still had to do the asking part.

Knowing that I had to stay from the very next day, there was no option other than asking for the permission today itself. So as soon as I came back from the tuitions in the evening, I went straight into my father's room. Luckily, he was sitting alone reading a magazine. The atmosphere was absolutely perfect for a tête-à-tête.

Okay, tell me one thing- and please be honest. Are you feeling that I'm paying this *asking about the permission* thing more attention than required? If yes, you've developed my kind of understanding and if not, then you have the capability of reading any book in this world without getting bored. By the way, I'm doing it only because I want you to feel the excitement I was going through at the prospect of staying out with my friends.

'Good evening papa,' I said as I assembled myself on the chair in front of the bed on which he was sitting, 'what are you reading?'

'Good evening, when did you return from your tuitions?'

'Just now, about five minutes back, so what are you reading?' I said getting closer for a better look of the cover page.

'Oh, this, *India Today*, you want it?' papa asked.

'Nope, not now, anyways what topic are you covering?'

'About the opening of an IIT in our state' papa replied simply.

What the hell? This IIT bug doesn't leave me even at this time. Whatever you are doing, whatever you are thinking, from somewhere or the other you'll across the three letters. As a student, I ought to have expected it but I'm quite bad at expectations and that too from myself, impossible dude...

The last thing I wanted at this point of time was papa discussing about my studies and as always, the thing I feared happened.

'Preparing for the IIT, right?' papa asked.

'Well...'

'You want to get into one of those, don't you?'

'Not exactly' I said. I was quite frank with my father on matters like these, and you don't want to lie to your father about getting entrance in one of the most reputed educational institutions of the country.

But the better part of this was that my father is the best in this world. Maybe half of the people around the globe think that and so did I. He usually understood what I meant, and so gave his valuable comments just as any true friend would.

'Why, not able to cope up with the syllabus?' papa said.

'Maybe but only to some extent, I'm not very interested in the subjects' I said.

'What? But you chose them yourself. It was you who said that science will be your subject at senior school' papa reminded.

'Of course I did and I'm not saying that I'm regretting it either, it's just that I've certain ambitions quite different from my peers' I said.

'And what kind of ambitions, may I have the pleasure of knowing?' papa asked.

'Yes, I want to do management.'

'Good, so shall I understand that the *IIT idea* is dump and dusted?'

'Not at all, I'm not a loser, I'll still try' I said.

'And what about the Boards?'

'That's it; I want to get enough marks in Boards to get me entry into a reputed college. Having said that, by no means I want you to infer that I'll not try to crack the competitive exams' I clarified.

'Okay, the picture seems clearer, so your first ambition from here on is to get good marks in Boards?'

'Of course.'

'Good then, try your hardest, you'll most certainly succeed, at least I'm happy that you are aware of the circumstances' papa said and this attitude of his is what I love. He appreciated my aspirations, and that's exactly what you expect from you friend, or rather your father.

In the discussion about my future plans, I quite forgot about why I had come here. Then the idea sprouted again in my mind, making me feel a bit tentative.

'Papa, I needed your permission.'

'For what?'

'About *going* to a friend's home.'

'Permission for going to a friend's home, strange, I must say.'

'Well that's not exactly what I intended; I mean I've to stay there.'

'Stay there?'

'Yes, Pranav's parents are going out of the city for some days and so he asked whether I could stay at his place for three nights' I detailed the situation.

'Oh, and Pranav isn't going?'

'No.'

'Why?'

'Tuitions.'

'Then call Pranav here. He can stay at our home rather' papa gave an alternative.

'No, that's not possible. He can't leave his home, he has to stay there' I responded.

'He wants only you to come?' papa asked.

'No, Raj will also be coming.'

'And how will Pranav be eating?'

'No idea, maybe he knows a bit to cook.'

'Okay, I've no problems unless you face any. But tell me will there be no problem going to school at morning?' papa said.

'No, school is at eight and I'll be coming back by half past six in the morning' I said repeating the explanation I had given to Raj during the football match.

'How many days you said?'

'Three nights.'

'Right, but try and make it productive, I mean your stay could be utilized for a bit of combined study as well. Nevertheless have some fun as well, it we'll be good for you and your pals' papa said.

'You are great papa, thanks a lot' I said almost hugging him. See, it was so easy, just made my father understand the situation and he agreed. That's why I call him the greatest dad in the world.

'By the way, from when you have to stay?'

'From tomorrow.'

'That means Sunday, Monday and Tuesday nights?'

'Yes.'

'Fine then, tell your friend about it.'

I did precisely what papa had told me to do. I called up Pranav and told that I had got the permission. He was quite ecstatic to hear the news and informed me that Raj was allowed as well.

'Great, so we are coming tomorrow' I said over the phone.

'Of course, you are most welcome.'

'What time?'

'Whatever might please you. I'll return from tuitions at about eight in the night, you can be here anytime after that' Pranav said.

'Right, see yaa.'

'Bye.'

******

Here is *actually* where the notion about writing a book began. No, I'm not saying that the idea sprang to me at this point; that was only after I had spent the nights. What I mean is that it was because of the school's sucking standards and the three nights that I've composed this piece. Nor had I got the permission, nor would have I stayed and nor would have I stayed, nor would I've written my experience.

Too many *nors?* Sounding bad? It's because I'm not an author by profession, I only wrote this tome because my heart wanted me to do it.

Papa told about his grant of permission to mummy at dinner and my mother didn't seem very pleased by that but after I had made her calculate about the positives that could be drawn, she finally agreed.

Right, I've been dictating the entire last week of my life because I wanted you to live the world from my eyes, because I wanted you to realize how I lived my life and by now I expect you to have understood that. Similarly I've understood your life, just ring me once whenever you want to know about it.

I could've started directly with my three-night stay but that wouldn't have been the ideal way to do it. Now, since most of you are already aware of our mode of living, let's get the game going...

From tomorrow is where I'll receive all the experience that secretly tempted me to create a piece of my own so that I can share it with you. Let's go to sleep now...

I always have wonderful dreams; hope you get a part of the pack this time around, *Sweet Dreams* folks...

# 9

# Start with a Sunday

My Sunday is never a Sunday...

Tell me what do you imply by a Sunday? Yes, a day you can relax, a day you can get time off for your favourite activities...

Just the contrast is the case with me. I've tuitions running down my neck from the very morning till the sun scorches down on my head in the afternoon. With the addition of the physics coaching at Dilip Sir's, the position was even more grueling. However, the thought of seeing some girls at my new tuition put me in a positive frame of mind. Further, tonight I had to stay at Pranav's place which I foresaw as an interesting job.

The chemistry class was quite fine with all of us enjoying ourselves along with concentrating on what was going on. You might already be aware of the characteristics of our teacher. If you have forgotten (which by no means you should), he was one of the best teachers I've come across all my life.

Chemistry was followed by mathematics and thus the change of teachers took place. Our math teacher was quite peculiar, with his *not so humorous* jokes he kept cracking all the time. Anyways, he had a full command of his subject giving us a reason to study at this place.

'Boy,' said Jai midway through our math class, 'I can't stand this. Six hours of continuous tuitions, my entire mind gets drenched.'

'So does mine, this is so cruel' said Karan.

'You know what- we work so hard in these two years that we should get entry into an IIT without any exam' said Shubham.

'Ha, what a joke' commented Vicky chipping in his thoughts. 'Everyone does this, so you say there should be about a hundred IITs in India accommodating everybody that takes up science at high school.'

'No, that's not possible' I said.

'Exactly, that's not possible but something else is' said Shubham.

'What?' Vicky asked.

'The educational system should be looked upon, and wholesome changes must be made. You see some of the developed nations, students don't have to worry about whether they'll get a job after college' Shubham compiled a gist on how the educational systems of other countries worked.

'That sounds good but it isn't easy' I said.

'Who says it is? People will have to work together and make this a better place' Shubham said.

'You think that. No one else does. Nobody cares for the nation's betterment, everyone is greedy' said Ravi for the first time.

Oh, don't get worried, we all sit together, and if you are thinking how the hell we are able to talk so much during a class, I must tell you that we talked all this in intervals and I'm not that good an author who can talk about the discussion giving regular hiatus from time to time.

'Yes, corruption here is present at the grass root level. You can't get any job done without offering some bribe. You've to pay even if you want to get your own money back' I said making all the people in my vicinity aware of the fact that I knew something about the place I dwelled in.

'So it's not the nation that needs to be changed, it's the mindset of the people' said Karan.

'And it's a tough job too' Jai said.

'Hmmm... good problem' said our math teacher halting our discussion about the plans to make India a better place to live in. And he wasn't talking about our problem, he was talking about Naman's; yes, our *confident-to-crack-the-IIT* Naman had given the educator a question and of course it wasn't easy; that's why the lad was unable to penetrate through it.

The question was from Calculus and boy, it is one of the most difficult parts of mathematics, from my opinion; others might find it easy. In fact, I find everything tough other than writing this thing. This is certainly the most interesting job I've found lately. Anyways, as I was saying, now we were looking with full focus on the board.

'So boys, anyone has an idea about how to proceed' our teacher added. He looked at us with an expression that said everything about what he had anticipated from us; he hadn't expected anything more than us keeping mum.

'Oh God, what have all you dupes learnt in these many days?' sir said. He usually addressed us by that name and I think it was quite appropriate for most of us excluding a few. We were poor; especially in this part of the business- dealing with problems, and it was for a reason- we considered these problems small; after all we had many bigger tribulations troubling the nation to be solved.

'Sir, we can try the L'Hospital Rule' Vicky prompted and I don't know what he had intended to do with the question scribbled on the board but who cares; at least he had said something, saving our impression to be deteriorated further in the teacher's eyes.

'Good, that's it, it was so easy, differentiate it once and you'll get the desired result' said sir and at once the brighter minds of our coaching started rubbing the tips of their pens against the paper and one would have known, Naman was the fastest.

'Right sir, got it' Naman said forwarding his notebook to sir.

'Good enough, but why weren't you able to solve it?' sir asked.

'Oh, didn't get the idea, moreover in the previous problems of this exercise, nowhere this rule was needed to be applied.'

'Naman, don't just go on solving questions after questions, give each problem individual attention, I hope you had tried this problem a number of times?' sir said.

'No sir, not many times.'

'That's your only problem, once you are unable to solve a question, you leave it for me. You need to get this mentality changed, and then surely you are up for it' sir suggested.

Unbelievable, even Naman wasn't entirely prefect, I thought. What would happen to me, then? IIT seems a far-fetched thing; will I be able to get entry into a half-decent college? It's not that I'm a loser, nor am I a pessimist, it's just that I've realized nothing comes easy at this place. There are enough competitors to punch and knock you flat on the ground.

After the math class, I had second day of my new physics coaching and as I've said before, I was happy at the prospect of seeing some girls there, especially the *sexy waali.* It was quarter past eleven on the clock at this point, and thus we had fifteen minutes for the third and final tuition of the day to commence. The physics coaching centre wasn't far-off, so we were confident on reaching on time on the second, if not the first day.

'You saw the girl who had come by a white Maruti that day?' Shubham asked.

'Nope, whom are you talking about?' I said.

'It's useless asking you, you were too busy wishing Shikha her birthday. Oh, I forgot about it totally, how was the party?' Shubham said.

'Oh yes, you didn't tell a word about it, did you even go to her place?' Jai asked.

'Of course I did' I said.

'And you didn't tell us anything about it? It doesn't mean you won't say anything unless we ask for' Karan said.

'Completely forgot about it just as you all had' I replied.

'That suggests not much happened' Shubham concluded.

'On the contrary, the birthday was excellent, much better than what I had hoped for' I said unable to resist a smile on my face.

'Oh, why was it so good?'

And I told them everything, maybe in brief, but I was pretty careful not to miss even the smallest part. From Esha's wide knowledge to the sweet kiss, from the discussion with Shikha's father to the ice-cream, I dictated everything. My storytelling didn't even finish when the coaching began.

'Fantastic, you did it man' said Jai patting me on the back so hard as if I had saved a bank from getting robbed.

'Lovely man, you deserve applause' said Shubham and all three of my friends slowly clapped so that the teacher couldn't hear. Anyways, we used to sit on the last bench.

Halfway though the class when sir was dealing with some *engineering-level* numerical, Shubham again spotted the girl he had seen the other day on a Maruti.

'Yes, I was talking about her' he said pointing his finger towards a girl who was wearing a blue *salwar kameez*.

'So what's the matter with her?'

'What's the matter? Nothing, fool,' he said, 'I'm just saying she's the one I was talking about before you started your dictation about the party.'

'Right, is she good?'

'Yeah, according to me, she is just about fine.'

'She looks a very decent girl to me' I said.

'That's what good about her; you don't want a girlfriend who has five other boyfriends' Shubham said.

'What?' Jai asked turning his face towards us. He has this habit, every now and then even if he's not listening to us, he'll turn up and ask you something showing that he's very interested.

'Nothing, out of your reach,' I said forcing him to turn his head back towards the board, 'I'll tell you later.'

'Oh, so my dear boy has gone as far as that?' I asked Shubham.

'What far? Be clear about what you are saying.'

'I mean you want her to be your girlfriend?'

'Which boy won't? I mean getting close with such a decent girl is a challenge' said Shubham.

'Is it? You remember you said exactly the same words to me about Surbhi?' I said.

'Yes, I did and it's cent percent true, don't you think?'

'Absolutely. Anyways, I've my thumbs up for the *decent girl'* I said stressing on the last two words. That's the way we usually address the girls if we don't know their names or even if we do, in some cases. There are loads of examples to make you understand, just like *sexy waali* or *decent girl* or *nurse*.

Our blabbering seized at this moment as we saw the teacher approaching us. The good thing about our discussions is that we manage to study even while talking, just as the case was now. We had dealt with the question he had given on board, or at least that is what I thought.

'So boys, you might not be getting very much but tell me, have you done anything?' sir asked peeping into each of our notebooks individually. All the four of us had more or less proceeded in the same way.

'Good, your approach is right unlike many others. However I must admit you haven't got the actual result as yet, try for a couple more minutes, you all are close' he said turning his face towards the boys seating adjacent to us.

'Cool, it's the second day and we are quite getting it' said Karan.

'Yeah, and that too both in terms of the studies and girls' I commented. 'So tell me Karan, chose anyone?'

'Nope.'

'Don't worry, you'll get one soon enough.'

'What's the use? Are we able to have even a single date with the girls we choose?' Karan asked.

'No, but at least we can spend whole of the year noticing them, something that keeps you motivated not to miss a single physics class' Jai said.

'Yeah, right you are. That's not the case with the other classes, I can't keep on coming to see *nurse'* Karan said.

'I told you, don't call her by that name now, she was really hurt' I reminded.

'Oh, sorry, just forgot' Karan apologized. This is why these boys get going so well with me, they understand me. Someone else might have inferred some other meaning by my statement given just above.

We were more than happy when the physics class for the day drew to a close. Finally our hectic load of three continuous tuitions subsided and all of us looked forward to a better second-half of the day.

'Shubham, I failed to remember one thing, I had to ask you something' I said as the two of us proceeded to our homes. Jai and Karan, as you might know, had already departed to their places.

'What?'

'I'm staying for three nights at Pranav's home along with Raj. Pranav was wondering whether you could join us' I informed.

'Aaahhh, would've loved to but you know I can't.'

'Why?'

'Oh, don't you remember? I'm going out of the town for a week. I had told you, you are forgetting quite a lot these days.'

'Am I? Yes, you had said about yourself going to attend your cousin's marriage ceremony, right?' I guessed and I was spot on.

'Of course, at least you remember that.'

'Great memory I have, isn't it?'

'Yeah, by the way should I talk to Pranav about it?' Shubham asked.

'About what? Regarding your unavailability, no need, I'll be informing him' I said.

'Sure?'

'Absolutely, attending your cousin's marriage is more important that camping out at night with your friends' I said.

'Frankly, the second option is much more tempting but as you say, going to the marriage is important' Shubham said as we neared the place where lanes to our homes separated.

'So you wouldn't be coming to school for a week?' I asked.

'No, it would be awkward missing the entire week when you know this school fucks you if you've attendance problem.'

'Right, but you can't do much about it, can you?'

'No, right then, see yaa later.'

'Yeah, after a week, will be missing you' I said.

'So will I, keep SMSing at least.'

'Sure, and happy journey.'

'Thanks, bye.'

'Bye.'

******

The afternoon was dull and so I opted for napping and compensating for previous night's less amount of sleep. In the evening, Rebu dropped at my place as he was returning from his tuitions.

'Hi, what's up?' he said, 'wake up.'

'Oh, what... Oh, Rebu... when did you come?'

'Right now, didi said you were sleeping and so I thought of chipping in directly' he said. I think it's quite ironical that Rebu used some football terms in his day to day life, just like *chipping* and *crossing* and *using your head*.

'Oh,' I said rubbing my eyes as I sat up on the bed, 'what's this?'

'This? Bro brought it from London' he said as he gave me a clearer look of a beautiful blue bag that shone as if radium was fitted into it. On middle of the bag was the crest of the Chelsea Football Club.

'Ah, lovely' I said spotting the logo. 'Why didn't you tell him to bring Arsenal's?' Arsenal was the team we both supported, or we were rather die-hard fans of it.

'I said the same thing, he just brought it as a gift, and he didn't ask me.'

'Never mind, it's wonderful.'

'Yeah, that's what matters. Anyways, I want the NCERT chemistry book for a day. You have it, right?'

'Yes, I do.'

'You have to study?'

Until now, I didn't have to study but as soon as Rebu put forward his question, I wondered how much I could I've studied in a day.

'No, not really.'

'I've no problems if you have to, I'll be taking it later' Rebu said.

'No, you need it for how many days?'

'I'll be returning it tomorrow evening.'

'Take it for sure, anything else that I can do for you, sir?'

'I don't think so, not at this point, just escort me to the end of the lane.'

'You are leaving?' I asked, surprised by Rebu's sudden change in plan.

'Yeah, I'm supposed to reach home directly after tuition. However, we can talk for sometime on the street.'

'Of course, just let me find my sandals.'

'Sure.'

We talked for about half an hour on the street on various topics the last of which was about the TV serials.

'Rubbish, this *Saas Bahu* stuff has gripped the nation, it's so boring, in fact it wastes so much of the valuable time of many people' Rebu said.

'It's amazing how woman especially *mummy types* can bear it' I said.

'They don't bear it, they love it. According to them, these serials represent the ideal family.'

'What the hell? That's ideal? With people marrying twenty times in a single life, I don't think that's close to what people call *the right way to lead a family...'* I said.

'These TV soaps are like that, there are very few channels in India that provide actual entertainment, just like AXN.'

'Yes, that's a fascinating channel, I adore it. So many serials, Fear Factor to Ripley's, everything's superb' I provided my thoughts.

'They show magnificent things, yesterday they showed about a woman whose face was entirely silver in texture, as silver as the metal itself,' Rebu said, 'they said it was due to an extremely rare disease which was in full flow in her body, it was unbelievable.'

'Unbelievable indeed,' I said, 'Discovery and Nat Geo are interesting channels as well. One of them had done a story on Vampires, and not an ordinary one, they met people who live as vampires till date.'

'Really?'

'Yeah, they talked to a man who lives in England and can't live without human blood.'

'Strange... Oh, I completely forgot about the time, I'll have to leave' Rebu said.

'Dear me... I forgot about it as well.'

'Bye, we'll continue our conversation later.'

'Sure' I said as Rebu paddled his bicycle hard to make it reach speeds which it couldn't. In a fraction of a second, the boy along with his bicycle was out of my sight.

As soon as I returned home and closed the front door, the bell rang. It was Raj this time, looking delightful as always.

'Hi, come in' I said greeting him.

'Hi, just met Rebu, he was in a hurry' he said.

'Yeah, he got late talking to me, so he had to rush back home.'

'At what time will you be coming today?' he asked seating himself comfortably on my quite a *comfortable* bed.

'Tonight?' I said correcting him.

'Same thing. We've tuitions till eight, so would be coming after that' he said.

'Alright, I won't be coming at six anyways.'

'Okay then, I'll be coming at your place after dinner at about nine and then we can both go together' he said.

'Sure, but where will Pranav be eating?'

'Oh, at Zayed's place, aunty said she'll be feeding Pranav as long as he is alone' Raj said.

'Good, quite generous of her except for the *feeding* word, it sounds odd, as if Pranav is a cow' I said.

'Fuck you. She didn't say that, I only used it to make you understand, idiot.'

'So will Zayed be joining us?'

'No, you know how his parents are' Raj informed.

'Yeah, they are quite restrictive, but I thought knowing the situation they might allow Zayed' I said.

'What situation? Inviting Pranav for food and allowing Zayed to stay at a friend's home are entirely different areas' he said.

'Yup, you are right, by the way, Pranav asked me for some DVDs so that we can watch them' I said.

'Yeah, he said it to me as well, do you have any?'

'Nope, not anything new, we can ask Pappu if he has brought some.'

'Right, that's what I was thinking, I asked David as well, and he said he has some new Hindi movies' Raj said.

Pappu was the owner of a shop in our locality who gave video CDs and DVDs on rent, and he did much more than that. He sold anything and everything from earphones for IPods to recharge coupons of mobiles to mobiles themselves. His possession of a variety of goods made his shop one of the most recognized ones of our colony, and gave it a tag of a *multi-problem solver shop* as well.

'We can watch Hindi movies in our living-rooms also, so we should be asking for some different kinds of movies' I suggested.

'And what do you mean by that?'

'Kind of movies that we friends can enjoy together. Some English comedy films, for instance.'

'Yeah, good idea,' Raj agreed, 'we'll not be taking any today, I would rather want talking and then sleeping tonight, the football match has taken a heavy toll on me.'

'Tomorrow, then?' I asked.

'Yeah, sure, we can take some Hindi horror movies as well' Raj said.

'Yeah, but they are hopeless, I mean you will be laughing your guts out instead of being terrified' I said.

'And that's exactly what I want; a bit of laughing will help our cause. And don't forget to ask for English movies with some scenes, we can certainly do with that' he said.

'Of course we can be okay with some scenes, they only increase the sensuality of the movie but what on earth do you mean by *ask for?* You would also be coming' I said.

'Sure man, I'll be coming, but right now I'm going, see yaa at nine.'

'Right, see yaa.'

******

You know what- if I would've wanted I could have directly skipped from here to the scene where Raj returns to my place to take me to Pranav's house, but I didn't do it and there's a simple reason for that. Two continuous dialogues with the same person are not what a good author will want to do, and that's exactly what I've tried. So in between I'll talk about something else, or rather someone else.

You remember Kumar Uncle, I bet you do... I said he'll be staying in the town for a week and that's not over yet.

'Good Evening, Arjun,' uncle said,' 'have seen very less of you for the last two days, you are busier than I expected.'

'Oh, am I? I think it applies more to you than it does to me' I said. 'You are the one who is involved in important meetings and stuff.'

'Work comes first dear; anyways I've brought something for you.'

'What?'

'Wait here for a minute, I'm coming' uncle said and proceeded towards the dining hall. Oh, just to make you understand, my bedroom was the place where our conversation was taking place. I waited with anxiety thinking hard about what surprise uncle could possibly have in store for me, and it unfolded soon enough.

'Right, take this' he said handing me the most beautiful football I had seen all my life, I mean the most beautiful football I had witnessed in reality, I've seen hundreds like those on television.

'Whoa...what... cool... itttt's fabulous... thanks' I said taking the ball into my hands. It shone brilliantly and it was light too, lighter than a tennis ball. Oh, have I just gone a bit too far, I mean a football can never be lighter than tennis ball. Whatever, it was nice to put my *hands* on the *foot-ball*.

'Like it?' uncle asked thinning out his eyebrows

'Like it, I love it, thank you so much, you really know my taste, but tell me, it really would have cost you big money.'

'It's not that what matters, it's whether you are happy or not.'

'More than that uncle, I love you' I said as I saw mummy observing me from a distance of five meters and I think I saw tears in her eyes. Unbelievable, mummies get so much soaked in emotions even this time of the day.

'Give him more gifts,' mummy said approaching us, 'you are destroying him further. As if he was studying long enough that this was needed.'

'This is his age to play' uncle said.

'And his age to study' mummy said.

'No, I'm sure he'll excel in studies, the boy will put our names on top of the world' uncle anticipated.

It was good that he had brought me such a nice gift and he spoke such lovely words, but was he expecting a bit too much from me? After all, this *top of the world* thing stinks, sure I would like to do that but there is just so much sarcasm involved into it.

'Won't you, Arjun?' uncle said.

I...yaa...why not? I mean sure...' I fumbled for words.

'Be confident man' uncle said.

'Yes, sure... I'll try my best to succeed, think positive mummy' I said.

'That's the way, just keep going.'

'Yeah, just keep going... away from the studies' mummy muttered as she forwarded her steps back towards the kitchen.

'Don't mind, she just wants you to be the best, after all this is what all parents desire. She sees her reflection in you' uncle said after mummy had left.

'Yeah... absolutely... I want my parents to be happy as well, I'll be trying, uncle' I said.

'Right, but right now show your football to your friends; ask if their uncles have given them any such gifts.'

'Ha... not all uncles are like you, sir' I said.

# 10

# The First Night

I never thought waiting for Raj would be such a monotonous job...where the hell was this lad?

It showed quarter to ten on the clock and he still wasn't here. Mummy was getting increasingly worried about the fact that it was getting late and she didn't want me wandering on the roads at this time.

'Where is your friend?' she asked.

'Dunno... he said he would be here by nine... his phone is switched off as well.'

'I'll not let you go if he doesn't come in ten minutes' mummy warned.

'Oh c'mon mummy, I'm not a kid. Besides he'll be here in two minutes' I guessed and I would've done anything for my guess to turn into reality.

'Ting-ting......'

'Here he is' I said sprinting towards the door.

'Sorry... got late... dinner took time... mummy had forgotten that I had to leave' Raj apologized as soon as I detached the flap that closed the door.

'And I'm waiting for an hour now.'

'Sorry...'

'Alright, forgiven, stay here, I'm coming in two minutes' I said and went straight to papa's bedroom for bidding him good night.

'Okay, make it fast' said Raj with his voice echoing more than it usually would have.

'Bye papa, I'm leaving, see yaa tomorrow morning' I said.

'Oh... okay, good night, just call when you reach' papa said.

'Right, good night didi.'

'Good night bro, enjoy.'

'Mummy, don't worry, I'm returning within a few hours, good night' I said as mummy was seeing me with her eyes narrowed.

'Good night and take care' mummy said as I wore my slippers and took out my bicycle.

'I'll ride, you sit on the back' Raj said as he took the rider's seat. It's only ironical that people could load me on the back of the bicycles now; such was not the case a few months back-when I was about thirteen kilos overweight.

'There's some good news' he added.

'What?'

'Zayed is also coming.'

'Whoa... how did that happen? I mean how could his parents allow?' I said, taken aback to say the least.

'Yeah, that's what I was thinking as well, anyways does that matter?'

'Not really, the better part is that he is coming.'

The nights were relatively much cooler than the days and it was feeling good to be enjoying the fresh weather; I wished Pranav's home was farther but it wasn't to be- good things never last long- and that too with me especially. Again, the encouraging element here was that the second part was pleasurable as well...

'Hi Zayed, nice to see yaa' I said as both Zayed and Pranav came to open the front door.

'Same here, dude, why so late?' Zayed said.

'Ask him' I gestured towards Raj.

'Dinner was served late to me, forget that now, and let us enter.'

Pranav's home was not a very big one, in fact to be honest- it was really small but cute nonetheless. There were three bedrooms lined almost side by side with Pranav's being the middle one. I was quite used to enter his room straightaway and was doing the same today when the owner of the house interrupted.

'Come to papa's room, we were watching TV' he said.

'Oh... haven't been there before, let's see it' I said and entered the adjacent room.

It was more or less like my friend's bedroom; the only difference was that it contained a TV instead of the computer which I remember Pranav had got installed in his room after so many requests. Also, there was a common door to both the rooms which I had never seen open until today.

Zayed, Raj and I occupied the bed spreading our legs as if we were the people to whom this place belonged to; or did it? Maybe for these three nights, it did. Pranav made him comfortable on the only chair present in the room.

'So, what's the program?'

'Dunno... I'm already feeling sleepy' I said.

'What? Don't talk about napping now, we have only just come. Look at the time, it's only half-past ten' Zayed warned in a tone that resembled growling.

'I've bought some cola, we can be taking it when you people want' Pranav said.

'Not now, after an hour at least, we've plenty of time' Zayed said. What did he mean by *plenty of time?*

Was this guy planning to wake up the whole night or what?

'Tell me, when have you planned of going to bed?' I said absolutely unable to resist my anxiety.

'At least till one.'

'Don't forget, we've school tomorrow' Raj reminded.

'Point' I said.

'But we'll not be getting opportunities like this everyday, make it count once we've got it' Zayed put his notions to the force.

'Point' Pranav said in a voice louder than in which I had spoken the same word. Do you have hell of an idea what does this imply? Yeah... it says the second point was more valid.

'Alright, whatever,' I said, 'but tell me, what are we up to now? I can't spend three hours watching TV.'

'Nor can anybody else, just let this show finish, I love it' Zayed said and I looked up to the television set just to see what was he so desperately enjoying- it was a show in which a famous director interviewed celebrities. This time his guests were Vijay Mallya, a dominating Indian business tycoon and Shobhaa De, a lady journalist, I guess.

The businessman talked about his plans to make his brands a global one and similar crap. But one thing that he said was particularly interesting- he wanted to do things that would help India in its betterment; not many *Richie Rich's* talk like that, do they?

On the other hand, the woman conversed about how the lifestyle of the populace in India had drastically changed from conservative to what we may call dynamic. She spoke about the transformation in the number of people who lived the *Page 3* lives in the last few decades.

All and all, it was not such an attention-grabbing show, and I was glad it had finally finished.

'Oh, good it was, wasn't it?' said Zayed.

'What... right... quite good...' I said just for my friend's sake.

'Now, what should we do?' Raj asked. 'No more TV, surely.'

'No, no TV now, what about playing a bit of carrom, it has been ages since I laid my hands on it' Pranav gave an idea.

'Cool. Though I must admit I'm bad at it, so if we are going to play forming pairs, my partner should be a good enough player so that we have some competition' I warned.

'None of us are good at it either, and we haven't played it for a long time as well' Zayed said.

'Great, then we could be in for some *cheap-quality* but *competitive* games' Raj said.

The clock at this point of time showed twenty minutes past-eleven and I had no idea how long we were going to play, but as Zayed had said, these kinds of opportunities are rare and so we should make maximum use of it. I, therefore, had my thumbs up for anything.

Zayed and Raj formed a pair and so did Pranav and your very dear narrator. We were uncertain about how to divide ourselves and so we applied a very despicable logic; both Zayed and Raj had their pet names starting with the letter S, and so they were in one team.

Clearly, after a game or two, we realized the best player among the four of us was Zayed, and the worst one was Raj, of course. He is not one bit good in these kinds of things, still he has something in himself that makes him attractive, gives him that masculine look that every boy teenager has a desire for.

So, as expected, the left two candidates were average players and hence we did have a very close match. Our way of winning was simple; whoever reached twenty-eight points first would prevail. After an enjoyable period of two hours involving nine games, both the teams were tied on twenty-five points.

'Let us take some break, have some cold-drink and then again we can play' said Pranav and forwarded his steps towards the kitchen.

'Right, what an enchanting encounter, I've enjoyed every bit of it' Zayed said.

'Nice...' Raj said.

'What nice?'

'Alliteration was perfect; *enchanting encounter,* anyways the games were lovely, great player you are, Zayed' said his partner.

'And so are you, dude,' said Zayed with a silly smile, 'it was because of you that we won the last game.'

Yes, it was true; though Raj was not much more than an ineffectual player, he sometimes hit shots that even a professional would be proud of, and what was better- he hit those at precisely the right time.

'It was just a fluke, I didn't mean it' said Raj innocently.

'Whatever, that barred us from winning the match and that's all that matters' I said as I saw Pranav coming with a bottle of cola that I supposed to be of two liters.

'Man, help me, the glasses will fall' said Pranav desperately as he laboured hard to keep the four glasses in control. The remaining three of us did try and help him but it was to no avail; the glasses fell and what was worse- the glasses were made of *glass*.

*'Crack.........'*

*'Aaaahhhhhhhhhh.......'*

'What happened?'

And we looked down to find out what actually had happened. Not much; one of the glasses had plunged vertically on Pranav's toe and it was sprouting blood as if a municipality tap leaking water.

'Thank god, they make bottles of cola from plastic' Raj said with a childish smirk on his face.

'You are thinking joke? I'm hurt so badly and besides I've broken a glass set mummy bought last week' said Pranav quantizing the mistake he had just committed.

'Sorry...but it was funny.'

'Now what?' I asked blankly.

'Nothing, get your toe some antiseptic till we clear the pieces' said Zayed. He was always so practical; he was the man you would go to when you are in some dilemma. He doesn't talk about nonsense stuff and gets straight to the point.

'Wait. Before you go and get your toe some *dettol-treatment,* just answer my one simple question' Raj said.

'What?'

'What on earth did you think before bringing these glasses? We would have been absolutely fine with goblets made of steel' Raj growled.

'I didn't get any, and further I wanted to have cola in some *style'* said the boy with the injured toe.

'Great, now you can have it in style, with a beautiful toe sprouting red liquor' Raj said.

'Man, get hold of it, we've still games left, and I'm not sleeping until we complete those, so just joke around a bit more if you want to be awake all night' warned Zayed. One thing was clearly noticeable about this six-foot lad (yeah, Zayed was much taller than the rest of us) - he gave a lot of warnings.

'Yeah, be fast dude, go and get your foot alright, we'll clean the floor' I said and was off from bed at once for the boring job ahead.

It took five minutes of our combined effort to make the floorboards look like before again. We collected the glass pieces in a small bowl, and kept it in the kitchen, as we found no place to dump those. Meanwhile, Pranav had taken care of his foot and was up again for completing the left games.

'Here,' said Raj, 'here are the steel glasses, and you said you weren't getting any.'

'Fuck you. Just bring it and get us the cold-drink, and be fast' said Zayed.

I had never imagined that I would be playing carrom and drinking cola with my friends at half-past one in the morning. Moreover, we were in the twelfth class; a class in which you are supposed to get your act together for building up your future. We weren't close to that...

However, something else was building up- a dramatic climax to our match. Our opposite team was just one point away from a hard-earned win when Pranav did something incredible; he sent three of our white pieces into the holes in a single shot.

And we won...

We had reached twenty eight points...

'Whoa.....'

'Oh...... what... how...'

'My champ is here' I said still not able to believe what I had just witnessed.

'Thank You' said Pranav standing up and giving us a deep bow.

'How did you do that?'

'Stroke of luck,' said Pranav, 'how the devil did you think I could do that intentionally?'

'No... but still fabulous.'

'We did utilize time in a good manner' I said.

'Yeah, in fact we double-utilized it after a finish like that' said Zayed. 'But now what?'

'What do you mean by that? We are sleeping, aren't we?'

'I don't think we are, let us do something else, I mean let's make the nights worth remembering for the rest of our lives. Right?' he said asking for an immediate response from Pranav and Raj.

'Dunno, we've to go to school tomorrow, I think' said Pranav.

'Forget that. We can sleep in school, especially in ours. It's better napping the whole time than listening to the dumb teachers' said Raj.

'Irony... *listening to dumb teachers*' I said. 'I still don't think it's the best thing to do.'

'Please' Zayed pleaded.

'Hmmm, okay' Pranav said musing a bit over his decision. 'But what are we going to do?'

'That's the only thing left to decide' said Zayed. 'You got any idea, Arjun?'

'Dunno, I wonder what if some ghost, some banshee drops in, it'll be a lifetime experience, and that's what you want Zayed- something that you could remember for the rest of your life. Believe me, you'll remember it after death' I said.

'Yeah, nothing less than fascinating it would be' Raj added.

'What rubbish are you all talking about?' Pranav added.

'Afraid?' Raj imitated the possessor of the house, 'don't be scared, young boy, we'll save your ass from getting fucked.'

Zayed and I couldn't help ourselves from laughing our guts out on Raj's vibrant yet delicate replication.

'Oh, will you? But who'll save you from me?' said Pranav getting hold of the collar of Raj's shirt. He gave him a fake slap on his chin and the acceptor acted as if he was in immense pain. Then, as expected, both were rolling on the bed next moment.

*'Dus bahane kar ke le gaye dil...'*

'O-ooohh....'

'Who's calling at this time?'

'Dunno... I can't imagine anyone calling at this time of the night, it's almost two' Pranav said as he budged himself to the next room to receive the call. The telephone was a wireless one, so he brought it to us.

'Who's that?'

'Boy, I don't know this number, should I dismiss it?' Pranav asked complementing his question with a gesture involving his eyebrows.

'No, you shouldn't, show me the number', Zayed said with such authority as if his brain was a telephone directory and he knew every number of the town.

'Hmmm... it says 9292360123, are you sure your parents are not calling?'

'No, why would they be calling at this time?'

'Strange... let's switch on the speaker, we'll all hear' I suggested.

'Right, and be fast or else it will cut off' Raj said and reached out for the button which read the word SPEAKER in big bold letters. 'Should I?'

'Yeah' all of us said together but I think Pranav's voice was the faintest of all.

'Hello' Zayed said in a loud and clear voice.

There was no reply.

'Hello' our big friend repeated.

Again, there was no reply.

'Who's this?' Zayed was beginning to lose his temper.

'Hello' a deep and rusty voice echoed from the other side. The accent of the caller was so cavernous that we were all taken aback, even Zayed.

'You have no idea?' Zayed gestured to Pranav and the response was simple- a shake of his head concluding that even he was unaware about the initials of our *caller-calling-at-two-in-the-morning*.

'Yeah, what do you want?' Zayed said trying to keep his voice as bold as he could.

'Ha ha....' and there was a shallow laughter terrorizing us even more. 'Do you think you can provide me what I want?'

'This is getting interesting' Raj said in a relatively low voice.

'What? What did the boy just say? *It is getting interesting?* He feels so, ha, do you have the slightest knowledge to whom you are talking to-'

'Keep quiet, please' Pranav signaled to Raj.

'-you will urinate in your pants if I tell you all my real identity' the voice added from the other side.

But, as Raj was saying, all this was getting *interesting*. Yeah, there was an element of fear involved in our little brains but it was nothing less than adventurous, and much more than what I had expected. I mean, sure, I had anticipated some fun hanging out with my friends but all this was getting just a bit more tentative, or rather *funny*.

'Tell me, what do you want from us?' I said trying to show I wasn't feared by the slenderest of chances.

'Oh, other big boy rising up, hmmm, really bold you people are.'

'You fucker, be fast, or else it'll not take much out of me to beat you like hell' Zayed growled which were clear signs of him losing his cool. But, this was certainly not the right thing to do, not unless you are aware of the identity of the man speaking from the other side.

'Boy, I'm afraid, just hang around there the four of you. I'm coming, and you, beat me like hell' the voice was even more intense, at least to the level which prompted Pranav to keep both his hands in front of his mouth.

'Sorry,' he said, 'he didn't mean that.'

'No, I did' said Zayed. He was surely all fired up by now, and believe me; I've seen him actively involved in some of the most reputed fights that have taken place in or around our school.

'How do you know that there are four of us?' Raj inquired.

'I know many more things, don't worry. I'm dropping at your place in ten minutes, let's see what your big friend can do' the man said and I don't know whether it was my observation or bits of fear churning inside me, that I felt his voice was getting grimmer with every statement he spoke.

'C'mon, bring your fucking ass here dude, none of us are afraid of you, see me once, you won't dare to see me again' Zayed was boiling hot like water which is put at high temperatures in the latest microwave ovens you see in the elite's kitchens.

'Sorry, we are damn sorry', said Pranav pinching Zayed's thighs to keep him quiet. 'My friend is just a bit short-tempered, you see, what do you want from us?'

'Ah ha, the big boy says you people are not afraid, but I think this boy might be leaking liquid from under his knickers' said the man.

'You rascal, don't dare speak like that, if you have got so much power in your ass, turn up at once, I'll be waiting for you, you rogue' our so called *big boy* said. I had never seen any of my friends raging like Zayed was doing now. I had a strange sensation- I was starting to feel *uncomfortable*- he could *kill* anybody at this moment, I was starting to feel *comfortable*- he could *kill* anybody at this time.

'Okay, you have kept many names for me, cool. I like your style of talking, yeah, even when you are sweltering as you are now' the other side of the phone said. 'You start with rascal and end up with rogue, they mean quite the same, you see.'

'You moron-'

'Good, anything more?'

'Come up at once; don't try to stray away from the topic. And don't try to hide' Zayed said.

'I won't. See yaa and your friends in a few minutes.'

'C'mon-'

'Sure, bye' the man said and disconnected the call.

Unbelievable...

On one side, our friend was really fuming as if sodium put into water (if you don't know the reaction, ask about it from your chemistry teacher and even if he is doubtful, boys, or girls, if there are any reading this crap, you are mistaken- the person you asked wasn't a chemistry teacher). On the contrary, as you might have noticed (I'm not sure you are as good as an observer as I'm), the man talking to us over the telephone was calm but he had that graveness in his voice which made him appear serious, or maybe fearsome as I must admit.

'Who the hell this could be?' asked Zayed finally lowering the decibel-level in his voice.

'Dunno, but why did you talk like that?' Pranav said.

'Then what should have I done- just listen to the guy?'

'Yes, I mean no, but you could have. We don't know who he was and thus there is great danger if he arrives.'

'What danger? I'll kick his ass like hell. Let's see…'

'Drop it,' I said after a long while surprising everyone including myself, 'do you think he will come?'

'Let him, I *want* him to come' Zayed said.

'Don't get carried away dude, we need to know first who he really is. You know, someone maybe playing pranks with us' I said.

'Dunno, but I don't think so' said Raj.

'And what makes you say that?' Zayed asked.

'You heard the way he was speaking; I mean no one could quite *act* like that, it was *real* for sure' Raj answered.

'Exactly, that's what I was saying' Pranav said.

'Whatever, now we can just sit here and wait' I said.

'No, that is not at least what I think' Zayed suggested. 'We should be out there waiting for the lad.'

'Now, please Zayed, get serious,' Pranav said, 'you know what you are saying? To be out there in the dark? What will the neighbours say; this is a residential area after all.'

'Yeah, Zayed, keep your cool, be yourself until he arrives' I said.

'What do you mean by that? *Be yourself until he arrives? Be someone else after that?*' Raj asked.

'No, didn't mean that, drop the hell out of it, and just wait. We'll see what happens' I said.

'Okay.'

Fifteen minutes passed and there were no signs of the man who had blackmailed us on the telephone. We were getting still anxious as the clock showed quarter past-two...

Now it showed half past-two...

Quarter to three...

'I think the dumbass isn't going to turn up, Arjun was right, somebody was playing monkeyshines with us' Zayed said.

'Yeah, maybe, so the episode must be forgotten, what should we do now? Should we take some rest?' Raj asked.

'If you want to' Zayed said.

'You aren't sleeping, then?' I asked.

'No ways-' Zayed was saying when the *blackmailer* remembered us again.

*'Dus bahane kar ke le gaye dil...'*

'Is it him?' my reflex made me ask the question.

'Yeah, it is' Zayed said switching on the speaker button so that we all could once again participate in the conversation.

'Hi, still up?' said the man.

'Afraid of coming here or what?'

'Noah, why would I be scared of coming to a place that I visit every second day' the voice said and it sounded better now, quite cheerful as if talking just after accomplishing a mission.

'What... every... what? You come here every *second day*?' Pranav asked, puzzled.

'I don't think it would be anything worth making you wait, should I tell you my real identity?' the man said or indeed, a boy said.

'Who are you?' we all asked collectively.

'Any guesses?'

'Would you be telling us who you are or should I be coming at your place?' Zayed said.

'Oh, my tactics...'

'Don't test my patience, boy.'

'Sure?'

'WHO ARE YOU?' we snarled.

'David' he said blankly.

'What?'

'How- David?'

'I can't believe it... how could it be you?' Pranav said.

'It is... your very dear friend David.'

'Good job man, you made us wonder' I said being the first to appreciate what he had done. Right or wrong, in truth he had added a flavour of fear in our wits. He had given us an hour of anxiety, an hour of adventure, and an hour of apprehension...

'David? Can't be... how you made your voice sound like that? I mean you sounded like a professional blackmailer man...' Zayed said.

'Thanks for all your compliments,' said David with bits of excitement and laughter mingled in his reply, 'you still aren't aware of all my talents. That was easy for me; slowly you'll come to know about them.'

'Now dude, don't blush. Anyways, fine work, you most certainly spoke well, but why did you take so long to call for the second time?' Raj quizzed.

'Oh, actually, I slept, which I had intended in no ways. Nevertheless, my naps keep breaking at intervals and so I called after quite a while.'

'Great, tomorrow you are going to school?' I asked. David was not in the same school as we were, as you might have inferred. If you hadn't, no problems; either ways you know the situation now.

'Yes, I'm. But you all aren't, right?'

'WE ARE.....'

'What? Then why aren't you sleeping?' David asked, shocked.

'Because an idiot kept disturbing us by calling at this time' I said.

'Oh, did I disturb you?' David said innocently.

'No sir, not at all, in fact you provided us the perfect pleasure we could have only dreamt of... now please shut up and end the call, or I'll seriously start addressing you by names which you won't enjoy listening to' Zayed said in his *chivalrous* style.

'Okay, cool man, *good nights*.'

'What?'

'Yes, I used the plural form; I believe there are four of you there?'

'Please don't crack these cheap jokes at this time' Zayed said. 'And go and sleep, you fatso.'

'You've no right to call me like that. Now I'm losing weight, I'm only eighty kilos now.'

'Oh, you have gone underweight' Pranav said.

'No problems, I'll be working on that.'

'Should I kill you?' Zayed said.

'No, no. I'm going, see yaa.'

'See yaa' said Zayed with an infantile beam that suited his big oval face.

'This boy is awesome' Raj said referring to David after the call was ended. 'We didn't once think of him.'

'Yeah, never, by the way I'm happy to know that somebody was just *joking*' Pranav said.

It was almost half past-three until when our discussion about David's prolific idea continued. Once it had ended, we were still unsure about what to do next. This is what was fantastic about these three nights- we were uncertain about everything except the fact that we didn't have to sleep. Though Zayed was also feeling lethargic by his active participation in the events that had marked tonight, he was in no ways planning to sleep even by the smallest of chances. Then, an absolutely *unbelievable* thing happened- this time my cell started ringing...

'What? Who's this now?' Pranav said with panic again making his eyes appear like slits. His forehead twitched, and he was again starting to look uncomfortable...

'I think it's David again, he just wants to fill up for his absence from here' Zayed said as I reached for my Motorola set kept on the table contiguous to the bed.

I was shocked at seeing the name which flashed on the tiny yet apparent screen of my set...

I was surprised...

It was a bolt from the blue...

A total shocker...

I watched the cell ringing with my mouth-opened...

'What happened? Why are you staring at your cell like that?' Raj asked.

'It's... it's Shikha' I fumbled.

'Who?' all the guys asked at once.

'Shikha, jackasses. You don't know her, I'll tell about her later. But why is she calling *now*?'

'Wow, we have heard her name for the first time and we are the ones supposed to know why she's doing this shit, strange' said Raj.

'Pick it up' Zayed suggested.

'Should I?'

'Yes, dumbo, pick it and ask for the reason' Zayed said. 'Weird circumstances to call your boyfriend-'

'-she's is not my boyfriend, err... girlfriend' I rumbled as I kept the phone on my ears.

'What... what did you just say?' the sweet voice of Shikha said.

'No... not to you... huh? Have you gone nuts? You know what time is it? Shikha, I can't believe it is you...' I said.

'Maybe, but tell me, were you waiting for my call?'

'Huh? At half-past three in the morning, you expect me to be waiting for a call, strange...'

'Oh, I thought you would, anyways you were awake?'

'No, how can you think of that? I mean I'm not a security guard on night duty. Girl, it's the mid of the night you are talking about' I reminded.

'I know, but how are you sounding so fresh?'

'Fresh? What fresh? I always sound like this, don't I?'

'You do.'

'Anyways, why did you call *now?*' I asked.

'Sorry, I know I shouldn't have, but you forgot something.'

'What?'

'You don't even remember now?'

'Nope' I said and I was so deeply involved in the conversation that I didn't notice that Raj had gone and switched on the TV in full volume.

'What is that?'

'Oh, friends are just watching TV.'

'What?' she said with such surprise as if I had accepted a murder crime in a court. 'Your friends are watching TV? Where are you?'

'Oh... no... no... you heard it wrong, I said I was watching the serial *friends*.'

'Oh, did you? Even that is incomprehensible' she said.

'And you calling at this time is comprehensible?' I asked.

She didn't say anything...

'Oh, sorry, did I hurt you? Sorry, just didn't mean that' I apologized.

'No problems, but you are at home, right?'

'Yeah, where else?'

'Then tell me, why did you switch on the TV?'

'Just a mistake' I said casting an angry look on each of my friend's faces, especially on Raj. He was the one who had forced me to give answers to some of the world's most rubbish questions...

*'Are you with your friends?'*

*'Where are you?'*

*'Why did you switch on the TV?'*

What the hell...

*Will anyone please tell me that what on earth had she though before dialing my number?*

I dare not ask her, she might get the feeling that I didn't enjoy her idea of disturbing at this time of the night, which I must admit with full honesty that I did.

'You know why I called you?' she asked. I was getting increasingly perplexed with the complexity of the reason which had made it compulsory for Shikha to bother me now, and I wanted to know the cause. Having said that, I needed to be careful, careful of everything I spoke, I could not afford to say something silly again and then face irrational questions banged one after another.

'No, I said I don't, I can't guess it' I answered.

'You don't remember what you forgot?'

'No, really don't, sorry if I'm missing something important.'

'You are.'

'Tell me what, please?' I begged.

'Do you know what day is it?'

What the hell is this girl up to? Yes, by every means, I take pleasure in the time she converses with me, but that was not the case this time around. To be telling you the truth- it was rather embarrassing. You understand, in front of friends and all that, you have to answer some of the most silly questions, you have to take part in some of the most stupid discussions with a girl... it really is embarrassing... particularly when your friends are watching you with an expression that contains juvenility...

'Yeah, it's Monday morning' I said.

'And you promised me something?'

'I... did I? Can't remember... sorry... you tell?' I was utterly confused.

'You said you would meet me on Sunday.'

'Oh gaaawwwddd... of course... how did I forget?'

'Remember?'

'Yeah, I do.'

'But you didn't even call me' Shikha said.

'Sorry, I really am. You know, actually I was out with my parents' I lied.

By this time, all my friends were laughing madly at me but were quite careful to keep their decibel-levels down and I thank them for that. If it wasn't for my friends' this great effort, Shikha would have truly asked me a dozen more questions.

'But you could have called me' Shikha stroked a chord.

'Yeah... just didn't cross my mind, but was this the reason of you calling me?' I was amazingly amused at the cause explained by my friend.

'Wasn't it enough?'

Ha ha... the girl thinks the reason given by her for calling a boy whom she met after a year the week before at almost four in the morning is good enough...

What does she intend?

Will anyone explain me?

In truth, I've not yet realized what Shikha meant essentially. While writing this book, I tried to decipher the cause but was up with nothing. I think only girls can understand what they say...

So, I just want to request something to the girl readers (I hope there are some) - if anyone knows the genuine rationale behind Shikha's untimely call, please keep me posted.

I think I wander away from the conversations many a times. I just get absorbed by the thing which is on my mind. If it irritates anyone of you, I'm regretful for that. I'll try my best to keep the discussions continuous (which I'm cent percent sure I won't be able to)...

Anyways, let's get back to the exchange I was having with Shikha...

'No, I don't mean that' I said, 'you know, you could have called me tomorrow morning, evening, anytime except this.'

'I could have but then I couldn't have talked for free.'

'What?'

'Yeah, we both have network of the same subscriber, I guess, and it's free from eleven in the night to seven in the morning' Shikha informed.

This was indigestible...

For one, this was hilarious, or rather foolish...

And secondly, I couldn't help myself from the anger that forged in me when I saw the faces of my friends' red due to continuous mirth.

'Good joke. How do you think of these at this time?' I kept on reminding her of the fact that it wasn't a particularly good time to call your *boyfriend*...

I was her friend and was of course a boy, so boyfriend...

'It wasn't a joke. I'm serious.'

'Now c'mon' she really was talking too much.

'Oh man, I really am serious. I don't have any balance on my mobile, so I had to call *now*. Otherwise I would have called in the mornings or the evenings.'

'Really?'

'Yeah, that's the reason.'

'Whatever, by the way, I hope to see you soon' I said desperate to end the call.

'Will you?'

'Absolutely, I'll have to do something to make up for my mistake.'

'When?'

'You say?' I said.

'How would it be tomorrow?' Shikha forwarded her opinion.

'Tomorrow... err... okay...'

'Ah ha, thanks, but you'll be calling me, right?'

'Yep, of course.'

'You'll have to, I don't have any balance' the girl said.

'Right. See yaa, then' I said.

'Okay, see yaa, bye sweetu' she said.

'Bye what?' I was surprised. She was addressing me by what? Sweetu? Strange... of course she was the first girl to call me like that and I was totally bewildered (not to mention how many times she had shocked me already tonight).

'Sweetu, didn't you like it?'

'No, I mean yes, I did *like* it.'

'Then I'll be calling you sweetu from now on, okay?'

'Yeah, as you wish. Meanwhile, I'll find a name for you as well' I said.

'Will you?' she asked in a jolly voice. These girls are really impossible to understand. She sounded so happy as if she had won a million rupees in some TV show.

'What's the big deal in that?'

'You care for such small things, Arjun. This is what I like about you' she said.

'Fine then, see yaa tomorrow, bye!'

'Bye, good night!'

'Good night' I said and concluded the call which had thrown up so many surprises tonight. I had never in my dreams expected Shikha to call me at almost four in the morning and that too talk the way she did...

'Ah ha,' Pranav said as soon as I was back on the bed, 'you never introduced her to us.'

'Huh?'

'Why didn't you mate?'

'Because I met her only a week before. Not even a week, to be precise' I said.

'What?' Each one of my friends was quite flabbergasted.

'Yeah, only a week ago.'

'And she rang you up at this time' Zayed said. 'I mean even *professional* girlfriends won't dare to do this.'

'That's what I'm thinking too. And for your kind in information, she isn't my girlfriend.'

'Oh, really, why else will she call you s-sweety... err sweetu then?'

'How did you know that?' I was bowled over.

'Your phone was shouting! You have a Motorola set, right? It usually lets the people in the vicinity hear. Not bad, they would have built it like that for situations like these' Raj said.

'Did you hear everything?'

'No, not everything... fraction of the conversation, though I think we heard the interesting part' Pranav said.

'You all are assholes, you should have tried not to hear' I said.

'Huh? We should have not tried to hear such an interesting dialogue, why wouldn't we? But how come you have got so close with a girl whom you only met a week ago?' Raj was frantic to clear his confusion.

'What close? You are talking as if what the hell I've done with her. And to clear your doubts, she was in my previous school.'

'Goodness me... you know what you are saying? First you said that you met her only a week ago and now you are saying that she was with you in your previous school. What do you mean, huh?' Pranav said. He was the one who was doing most of the talking now; he is always so involved in the talks that contain girls. If you ask anybody in our circle for someone who knows and understands girls, each one of them will point their fingers straight at him.

I assume I could have tried to clear my most recent dilemma by asking him the reason for Shikha's inappropriate time for ringing me up, but I didn't and it was simply because I couldn't afford my friends to make a fool of me.

'Oh god, you people are *absolute* jackasses' I said. I had almost suffered equally when I was explaining Shikha's friends to Shubham and co. 'She was in the same school as I was previously but I didn't use to talk her to much. I ran into her in a party a week ago and we have talked quite a lot since then.'

'Cool, she's *almost* your *girlfriend* then?' Raj said.

'Dunno, not quite, she's just a friend I guess, but will you all please drop this topic out now, I'm getting rubbed the wrong way' I said.

'Alright' Zayed said and then we talked about how infuriating it would be to attend the school after a sleepless night, and how we would have loved to be absent unless there was no attendance problem.

The next two hours passed quickly enough with Raj imitating some of our teachers and though he wasn't great at mimicking, we laughed our guts out at the precise things he told us.

'How does the chemistry one teach? *You'll see ello colour comin' from the test toob, if you don't, you might have taken some other solt.'*

'The math one- *algebra is easy; I had completed it in three days when I was at school...'*

'Yeah, completed in three days,' I said, 'if he was so good, why didn't he clear the IIT?'

'Right, if he would have been such a fine student, at least he wouldn't have been such a third-grade teacher of a third-grade school' Zayed said.

'But the worst one is our computer teacher', Pranav said. 'That's why students boo him so much, I think he deserves it.'

'Most certainly does, I think some of our mates would have more knowledge than him, I dunno how the school appoints educators like these' Raj said.

'Yep, I think they have picked him from a *cyber cafe'* I said.

# 11

# Monday Morning

I had to amass all my self-strength in the morning to take a quick shower and get ready for school. "Really, this school stinks" I thought combing my hair. Wasn't it just pitiable that we blamed the school for all our misfortunes? Yeah, of course it was a place which was worthy of being loathed, but who would want to go to an academy after a night that contained absolutely no sleep? By the way, since I thought of all this while combing my hair as I've already said; let me tell you how my hair was like...

*'It's amazing,'* David used to say, *'it doesn't matter whether you comb it or not, it remains the same.'*

Once my English teacher had pointed out that to me- *'Boy, what locks you have got, it resembles a rhododendron bush.'*

I was immediately ready with the response- *'that's better, I'm happy it doesn't resemble a cactus plant.'* Her son was in the same class as I was, and he had converted his hair to *spikes.*

Even though I had been in the bathroom bathing longer today than I usually did, it showed absolutely negligible effect in the school premises. I had thought talking a long shower will allow me to be awake at the *boring place,* but it wasn't to be.

Only as soon as the second period which was math, I felt myself tempted to close my eyes. Pranav was fighting with all his wits to be awake as well, but he seemed to be in the same position as I was.

'Dude, I had told Zayed to take at least a bit of rest, my eyes are just not ready to open for five minutes' he whispered in my ears as the math teacher explained the rest of the class that he would be beginning *vectors* today.

'So had I,' I said, 'but he didn't hear once. Now suffer, he would realize how rubbish his idea was.'

'Not entirely, we did enjoy a lot.'

'And so are we doing here, *enjoying a lot*.'

I don't know what wave passed through me that I suddenly stood up and my mouth sprang out the words 'excuse me, sir.'

Pranav was staring at me with puzzlement, his mouth half-open, quite similar to the expression he had made when the phone had ringed the previous night.

'Yes, any problems?' the teacher asked in his usual high-pitched voice.

'Yep, y-yes sir' I still didn't know how the words were coming out. I think it were my reflexes which were handling the situation for me.

'What?'

'I wanna, sorry, I w-want to sleep.'

'What?' he sounded huskier this time and also the second *what* was louder than the first.

'Yes sir, I just want to sleep' I said as I saw the rest of the class cast me nonplussed looks. Whatever, I think it was for good; at least I was grabbing the attention of some of the *beauties* of the class, as Pranav used to refer to them.

'What are you saying, mister? Do you come to school for sleeping?'

'No sir, not for sleeping, b-but for building up the a-attendance.'

'What?' the teacher was ruining the effect with so many *whats*. And there is a simple reason for that- the educators here are good for nothing other than their subject (in some cases, even that wasn't the case). So, you don't expect anything more than a series of *whats*.

'Sir, actually I'm not feeling well, so I was just wanting your permission for keeping my head down' I said.

'Huh? What kind of students you people are, why do you come to school if you don't feel well, remain in your beds, there is absolutely no reason to come' the teacher said.

'HE TOLD YOU THAT WE COME TO THE SCHOOL BECAUSE OF THE ATTENDANCE PROBLEM' somebody in the class howled.

'Who said that?' the teacher howled even louder.

Nobody said anything.

'I'm asking who said that.'

Nobody uttered a word.

'I don't know what future these students have,' the teacher muttered to himself, 'and you boy, don't disturb the class in between, get your head down and sleep.'

'Thank you, sir' I said and sat down. Pranav pinched my thighs as soon I was back on my seat and I responded with a foolish smile. I think it was enough for him to be provoked to action.

Well, I hadn't exactly guessed what Pranav was going to do but he abruptly stood up, and said something.

'Excuse me, sir' Pranav's action was even more unexpected than mine.

The teacher, who was trying to make the class a productive one, was most certainly yet again hassled. 'Now, what happened to you?' he asked with frustration making his face appear worse.

'Sir, I'm feeling sick.'

'What the hell, do you think all this is some kind of a joke?' his voice was reaching extremities of aggravation.

'No sir, I'm *really* not feeling well' Pranav said.

'See, this is high level of indiscipline and I can take strict action if your behaviour remains like this, you people are absolute scoundrels, you don't come to school for studies' the teacher's face was red with anger, only a small needle-tap was all that was required to pour blood out of it.

'As if this place has teachers who can teach' Pranav murmured. In fact it was not only the teacher who was getting anguished; there were some signs of annoyance on Pranav's cute face as well.

The math teacher approached the last bench on which we were sitting (sorry, Pranav was standing at the moment).

'So, do you want me to be getting angry?' sir said. It's just my respect towards elders that I've addressed the teacher by "sir". Actually, he doesn't deserve it, not in his purest dreams.

'But sir, why will I want you to be getting angry, I just said I'm not feeling well' Pranav said and I think his answer was well justified. I mean, c'mon, why do you always want to publicize the matters? The tutor could have done with a simple "yes" or a "no", but he wanted to make something out of it. I don't know why the teachers here think that they are being targeted by the students, maybe their mentality has been developed to work like this.

'Okay, tell me, how's it that both of you are not feeling well at the same time?' the teacher interrogated.

'THIS IS FREINDSHIP' somebody in the class was doing monkey business.

'Sir, I don't know, it's a coincidence' Pranav said.

'Ah ha, coincidence, do you think so?'

'Maybe, it is infectious, yeah, I think it is infectious' Pranav suggested and this answer of his' was enough to get the class rolling. I don't know if the joke was that enjoyable, but that's what our mates found it to be. Unfortunately, the teacher was getting even hotter. I think it was *smoke* that I saw popping from his left ear.

'I know why people like you don't make it to anything. You just spend all of your precious time making fun of others and trying to impress girls,' (I saw some of the girls on the back-row giggling as he said this); 'your futures are dark.'

This was getting disturbing. Okay, he is the teacher and he ought to say things which can make us realize our mistakes, but in no ways he could decide our future. We all are quite grown up and are conscious of the efforts we are putting in; there is no need of people like these to demoralize us further. After all, it was our math teacher who was making issue of a small thing; good teachers would have either ignored it or handled it in a better way.

'Sir, I'm sorry if I angered you, just tell me whether I can put my head down?' Pranav was in no mood to further intensify the situation, especially when he was bereft-sleep for quite a long time.

'You do whatever you want, I'm in no mood to teach' said the teacher and walked out of the class. As soon as this happened, Pranav sat down looking furious with himself, which I suppose there was no need to be.

According to me, he hadn't done something as wrong as the teacher put it out to be. Anyways, who cares? Whole the class was showing thumbs-up to us for the job we had done, everyone was happy that they had finally received some respite from the long, boring and monotonous lectures.

'Thanks man, you have saved us' said Vicky patting Pranav on the back as if he had topped in the school exams.

Some of the girls also looked at us and smiled, but I assure you none of them who belonged to the *beauties'* group appreciated Pranav's efforts.

There are some things that I love about the school and the teachers here. Let me explain you with an example- the teachers at this place are utterly true to their words. Once if they say that they aren't going to teach, that does mean that they are in *no mood to teach.*

Anyways, I found this *teacherless* stint a good opportunity to award myself with some rest; at least I could enjoy some sleep till the next teacher arrived. So I kept my head down. I thought I was acting smart, but Pranav was smarter. He was already half-asleep by now.

I don't know whether I had slept or those were thoughts hovering around my sleepless brain, I was starting to imagine many things. Surely I wasn't enjoying a succinct nap; and I could be so certain of that because these notions were not same as the usual dreams that I used to experience. You are aware of those, aren't you? But, these thoughts were different, very different from the customary castles in the sky I used to practice.

Now, neither am I an internationally acclaimed theorist nor a conventional writer; so maybe I might not be able to communicate the feelings that struck me like a chord that day, but I believe that each one of you will in some or the other way comprehend my ideas.

I don't think the previous night was exceptional in any ways if you keep out Shikha's call; I'm sure there would be very few readers of this book whose boyfriend or girlfriend call at times similar to Shikha's. But if there are, your relationship is one that is impossible for me to figure out. C'mon boys and girls, there are better periods during the day to ring your mates up.

I told you-this habit of mine is very tough to stamp out, even when I've tried to do it. I always wander away from where I originally am. You can see it for yourselves- I started with the feelings that popped in my little head that day and now I'm discussing times for you to ring your pals up.

As I have just said a few paragraphs before that there are some things in this school that I liked, I must inform you of what those *things* actually are...

I'm happy that I left my previous school to join the *boring place*. Yes, of course, it is a boring place and all that, but it has made me realize that life is something which you can't take for granted. This place allows you to open up, it allows you to understand the very essence of competitiveness, and it allows you to follow the fact that you have to be always ready for anything and everything.... and it does that applying a simple logic- it gives its students so many problems in a short span of time that the pupils are sterner, more complex and are ready to face the world as it comes. No, don't worry, my hate for the school has not reduced, in fact it has *grown* to such a level that I'm forced to enumerate my feelings in such a way.

I was very much secluded in the school where I was previously because it did everything for me, it didn't make me tougher, nor did it allow me being self-dependent...

Well, what things lingered around my head that day are quite different from what I've told you till now, but they are quite similar nevertheless.

I felt the monotonous schedule of my life broken, I felt that I was free from the pressure of the family and the society to perform, and I felt free from my own demand to do something in life, to be successful...

You know what- there are flaws with the whole system of existence on this planet and that has awful results. We don't allow ourselves to live our lives to the fullest; we are the ones who are responsible for making our lives worthless. It is no one else but we ourselves who don't allow are minds to develop to its true potential, because we get satisfied with little progress. Though I must make clear that by saying this I don't intend you to understand that we shouldn't be happy with what we possess, but what I want you to understand is that we shouldn't stop dreaming, and thus, we shouldn't stop achieving...

One night with my friends allowed me in recognizing my fundamental thought of flying in the sky and I'm pleased I apprehended a basic law- the path to your goal doesn't matter, few ask for it, but what matters is whether you reach your goal in this big-city life... however, the path should be one which doesn't hamper your family's progress, it should be one which doesn't let your neighbour get poignant, which doesn't make the society get gloomy and which doesn't make your country get miserable...

Well, do you think I'm getting philosophical? If you are, let me make it very clear to you that I've no intentions to get into an idealist's point of views, rather I'm writing what I felt in that petite period of time in which my friends assumed me to be sleeping. Yes, these thoughts came naturally to me and I'm trying to connect it to you in the best way I can...

Some of the great people have said that we should live our lives being optimistic. Maybe I've no rights but I'll disagree on that notion to an extent. I tried to resist myself from the point of discrepancy but just couldn't. My heart just forced me to write...

Be an optimist, but don't be an absolute one...

Be a pessimist, but don't be an absolute one...

We need to find a balance...

If you are totally positive in your approach towards life, you'll miss many things. You'll not think of defeats and thus you'll not wonder about the reasons which enforced you to get overpowered by others. And surely if you don't think about the reasons, you'll not develop, not develop into a better individual... and maybe you'll lose again next time...

And please for god sake, don't be a total fusspot, try and see brighter aspects of life...

One last thing which I'll want to say is for those people who think that this nation doesn't provide them what they want, this advice is for those who think spending the life in some other developed country is of greater use, this suggestion is for those who think they are blessed to have left the nation, I must tell you something- it is not you who is blessed, it is our nation which is blessed to have got rid from people like you...

Yeah, that's it...

Dear folks, I think I've told enough...

This is just the reason why I considered my first night stay with my friends a total success in spite of the fact that we experienced worthwhile problems next day because of no sleep.

Now, let's get back to my life...

The school went roughly the same way as it usually did (though no other teacher walked out of the class). I had my physics tuition in the evening and today there were only three of us, I hope you remember that Shubham was out of the town for attending his cousin's wedding. However, I was excited, not only because I would see *sexy waali* again but because I had also had a meeting fixed today with Shikha; I was always cheerful at the prospect of having to spend some time with her.

There is nothing important of what the teacher taught us that day, and I don't remember that one bit. But I remember something else, a challenge that Karan forwarded to me.

'Okay, today you talk to the *sexy waali*,' he said as we still didn't know her name, 'what say?'

'Huh?' I was trying to concentrate on what was going on the class. 'What did you say?'

'Talk to *sexy waali* today.'

'What is this? A request, an order or a petition?'

'A challenge.'

Jai wasn't listening to us; he was busy observing the pictures of the bikes that lay on the cover page of his new notebook.

'Ha, are you serious?' I asked. 'You are challenging me to talk to a girl?'

'Yes, I am. It's not that you have to just go and talk to her. You'll have to talk to her once she leaves' Karan said.

'Huh?' I was confused.

'Yeah, I mean you'll have to stop her in the middle of the road and then talk.'

'What are you saying? What if she goes by an auto or something, would I stop an auto?'

'No, she doesn't. She walks for about a kilometer till the crossroad comes, and then she takes an auto' Karan informed.

'Oh, good knowledge' I said.

'Yeah, that's Karan for you. Tell me, you accept the challenge?'

'Hmmmm... hell yeah.'

'Cool.'

******

We eagerly waited for the class to wind up so that I could test my skills and it did end soon enough. Meanwhile, Karan had told Jai all about the plan and so the latter was also keyed up to look at my performance.

'And don't forget to ask her name' Karan said as he loaded Jai and me on his bike. And then he didn't start the engine...

'What happened? C'mon, she'll get very far' I said.

'No, she won't, see, you can still see her, let her just get a little bit distant' Karan said.

'You start man,' Jai instructed, 'and be slow, she will automatically get far.'

'You know dude, I'm so fast.'

'Idiot, this man is' Jai muttered to me.

It took about a couple of minutes for Karan to reach the *sexy waali*; she wasn't more than five hundred meters from the coaching by then.

It was embarrassing to stop a girl walking lonely like this; I mean it does look odd when three people riding on a bike stop a girl on a street crammed with people, and what was worse- Karan had brought his bike to halt very abruptly.

Though I don't want to disclose her first reaction but since I share almost everything with all of you, I must admit that the girl was quite petrified to see us like this; sure this is what you expect from a decent girl in spite of her being miraculously sexy.

I got down from the Bajaj Avenger, and went straight to face the young woman. I know this act was very foolish of us or rather *indecent,* but what other option I had- after all Karan had challenged me to do this.

'Hi,' I greeted getting down from the bike and running straight into her, 'you study at Dilip Sir's, right?'

'Oh, yeah, I do' she spoke in a meek voice. My two friends were analyzing my feat with a great deal of interest.

'Actually, I had to ask you something. May I?'

She was acting quite timidly. Well, I guess that's what every girl will do when she is being exploited the way we were doing. I used the word *exploited* because she was really being used as a tool for promoting our interests, for us to have some fun.

'Yes' her voice was so weak that I had to put my ears very near to her mouth to make any sense out of it. I think she was thinking otherwise; maybe she was considering me a bloke who proposes every second girl every second day.

'Thanks. I have joined the tuition recently, I heard you study chemistry also there?'

'Yeah' she sounded better now, only relatively though.

'I had to ask how the chemistry tuition is, my friend is searching for it' I made up a reason in quick time.

'Well, it's good' she said. None of her answers contained more than two or three words. By now, one thing was very clear to me- most of the girls are a total contrast to their outer appearances. And she wasn't an exception; nobody would ever guess her voice to be so docile; maybe it was so because of the situation but docile nonetheless.

'Please be honest, after all my friend needs to attend a good coaching institution' I said, and I think there was some over-acting involved; I could make that out by looking at my friends' expressions.

'It's good; it really is' she said.

'And how's the teacher? Is he caring?'

'Do you need a baby warden or what?' she said smiling, or rather it was a sluggish kind of a smile, maybe she wanted me end the conversation. It was proved then-my acting wasn't just good enough. 'Sorry, yes the teacher is damn good; he'll be good for your friend.'

'Thanks' I said.

'What for?'

'For giving *heaps* of information, what is your name by the way?'

'Priya.'

Cool, sexy name of a sexy lady, I thought.

'Sorry' I said. 'Sorry for stopping you like this, I hope you didn't mind?'

'Actually, I did. Every second girl will. Please don't ever stop any other girl like this again, she might not like it.'

'Sorry again, please, I didn't want this to happen' I made an apology.

'Okay, shall I move on?'

'Yeah, sure' I said making way for her.

Unquestionably, this banter of mine with the *sexy waali*, err Priya, wasn't a total success but I didn't mind that until I had completed Karan's challenge. And anyways, I had more important things to look forward to- a *date* with Shikha and then there was of course the all important second-night stay at Pranav's home...

I'm not sure about one thing- about whether I can classify my meeting with Shikha that evening exactly as a date. Maybe yes or maybe no- I think you people who have worthwhile experiences are a better judge than I am.

There was one more thing that I was unsure of (my life is based on uncertainty as you might have realized by now)... I couldn't decide as if what would be the better option- going home and then calling Shikha or ringing her up from there itself so that I could summon her somewhere close by.

As far as fatigue was concerned, the second alternative sounded better and it was because of the fact that I need not go to home and could have directly moved to Shikha's meeting place but I didn't consider it. And again there was a very simple reason involved- I didn't want to call Shikha in front of my friends and then answer loads of stupid questions fired at me by my pals which one can't avoid... so I asked Karan to drop me at my place.

******

'Hello,' I said dialing Shikha's number.

'Hi' the refreshing voice of my friend boomed.

I was still an amateur at handling situations like these... hope Pranav was here... he could have surely been of some assistance to me but I was helpless... I didn't know from where to start; should have I asked- *so lady, ready for the date?* or *where do you want us to meet?* or *are you sure you can't do without us meeting today; I mean I'll learn how to talk to a girl by then...*

But I was lucky big time because it was not needed for me to initiate since Shikha commenced- 'You are free now, right?'

'Yeah' I said.

'So will *Rosetta* be fine for you?'

Rosetta... what Rosetta? Oh, I remembered-it was the name of the premier ice-cream parlour of the city.

'Yeah, I think it would be perfectly fine for me' I said calculating how much it would cost me to reach there by an auto. Oh gosh, I could not in my dreams imagine spending big money; after all David's birthday was just tomorrow...

'Fine then, see you in twenty minutes' Shikha said. 'You have no problems, do you?'

'No, none, it'll be a pleasure taking you out for a date-'

Oops! The word sprang out from my mouth without any warning; I had not intended to speak this out!

'Oh,' she almost teased me, 'so the big boy is taking me out for a date, are you?'

This was agonizing; I think the girl could have done without so much over-acting, I don't know why girls need to mix so much artificialness into their voice or maybe I was wrong, maybe it was just natural for them.

I decided to act smarter; I couldn't afford to behave like a rogue- 'of course young lady, you have no problems hanging out with me, huh?'

'No sweetu, I'll love to. You thought a name for me?'

'Oh... no... yes, I've thought of a wonderful name' I said.

'And what's that?'

'Why are you so impatient? We should have something to talk about when we meet.'

'Sure, see yaa in twenty minutes, then?'

'Right, twenty minutes' I said. 'Bye.'

'Bye.'

******

Various thoughts flitted around my wits during my short trip to the ice-cream parlour:

*Was Shikha getting too close to me?*

*Was she fancying me?*

*Did she enjoy my company just as I did?*

*Were all these thoughts just a result of infatuation?*

I couldn't find an answer to any of these and it didn't bother me very much. One thing was guaranteed- I was fancying her... or why else was I so obsessed with a feeling that told me to be in Shikha's company most of the time?

When I reached Rosetta, I found her already waiting for me at the front entrance; I say the front entrance because there was a door from the backside as well. Was she always so punctual or was it the delight she experienced in my companionship that forced her here so early?

'Hi,' I said advancing towards her, 'are you waiting for very long?'

'Oh hi, no, I've just arrived' she said and moved her feet towards me with such great pace I thought she was going to kiss me in public but no, I wasn't so fortunate... she hugged me... even that would do, I thought... at least she was happy to see me...

'Sorry I couldn't meet yesterday, these tuitions take a toll on me' I said making her realize the scarcity of free time in my quite-a-busy-itinerary.

'No problems mate, rather I should apologize, I acted insanely yesterday, and I mean what would you have thought?'

'What are you talking about? Your phone call?' I asked opening the door of the shop. The shop was already flooded with *other* couples.

Ah ha, don't think otherwise. The word *other* here by no means implies that we were one of the couples... it just tells you that the shop was very famous as a place where boys can take their girlfriends out for a piece of their favourite flavours.

'Yeah,' Shikha replied, 'you wouldn't have liked it, did you?'

'Absolutely I did' I said blankly.

I did not know whether I had spoken something as shocking as Shikha made it out to be- she stopped dead straight and stared me nonchalantly-'What, it didn't bother you?'

'Noah, and c'mon, stop behaving like a kid, you just wanted to call me and that's what you did, what's the big deal in that?' I said and truly, my hidden thoughts were just a total contrast to what I was speaking. After all, that's why they were *hidden*!

Though I've told you a hundred times before that chocolate was the ice-cream flavour I adored, but not such was the case at this place, here at Rosetta... here coffee was the one which I just loved licking... it was fabulous, and this was the reason why I accepted Shikha's proposal of meeting at Rosetta at once.

'What will you take?' Shikha asked as we neared the counter.

'Coffee flavour, I love it' I said.

'Oh, great, that's the one which I like as well; we have many things in common, I guess.'

'You've guessed right, we've everything in common except for the fact that I'm a boy and you are a-'

'-girl' she completed the sentence for me and started laughing. She looked so beautiful when small pimples made their way into her cheeks... it was awesome to observe locks of her hair falling onto her ears... she was growing increasingly irresistible to me... I just somehow stifled my desire to give her a wild kiss...

'Yes ma'am, what do you want?' asked the salesman breaking my fantasying chain of thoughts.

'Two double coffee cones, please' Shikha said and turned towards me. 'You know, you have become important to me in a few days, it just feels as if you are the best friend I can find on this planet to share my thoughts.'

'Oh... yeah... same here,' I said finding no other alternatives, 'I will always be your true friend.'

'Oh... t-thanks' she said and I think I saw a bit of disappointment in her eyes; I dunno what was that for?

'Well, I also want to tell you something' I said accepting the two big ice-cream cones from the seller.

'What?'

'I think a double coffee will cost more' I said with an idiotic smile to relax up the situation.

'Ah... you scalawag.....'

'There's a seat' I said spotting a table empty in the far-corner of the shop.

'Yeah, c'mon or someone else will latch on it' Shikha suggested and it was good to see a girl act like this. Do you understand what I'm talking about? I mean half of the girls would have replied otherwise to my three-line statement- *'we need not seat, and anyways, it's too far for us to go...'*

'Tell me, how are the studies going?' I asked as we settled ourselves on the huge maroon comfortable chairs.

'Hmmm... studies are just about fine, yours?'

'Same... just about fine' I said.

'So you have any girlfriends?'

'What... girlfriends?' I was surprised to say the least at the sudden change of topic. 'Yeah, but only one.'

'Who?' she sounded excited. 'Is she in your school?'

'Nope.'

'In your coaching?'

'Nope.'

'Then where, in your colony?'

'Nope, guess more' I said enjoying the circumstances. The ice-cream was doing enough for doubling the pleasure (after all it was a *double* cone).

'What guess more? She isn't in your school, not at your tuitions, nor in your colony... oh, have you found someone on the internet or what?'

'Nope' I said the word for the fourth time in quick succession. All this was adding to the effect.

'Please tell me, are you joking?' Shikha sounded desperate. I couldn't imagine people getting frantic in conditions like these... after all I was just teasing.

'No, I'm not joking' I said.

'Who is it then?'

'You' I said calmly; I was calmer than a spiritual book kept on a broken shelf at some corner of an old library.

'What... I... how could it be me?' she was stunned; more shocked than a common man who sees a politician working for people's benefit.

'Yeah...' I said as if it had occurred naturally to me.

'Are you kidding?' she asked.

'Yeah.'

'What?'

'Absolutely yes, good acting, wasn't it?'

'Oh gosh, you shouldn't have, I thought you were serious.'

'What if I was?'

'Oh... dunno... drop it man... we'll talk about it sometime later' she said ending quite a dramatic scene.

'Cool,' I said gulping the last bit of cone left, 'this place rocks. You want anything more?'

'No... one double cone is more than enough, should we move now?'

'Sure' I said approaching the counter for the payment.

'Wait,' Shikha said holding my hand, 'I'll pay.'

'Are you nuts?'

'It was me who called you here.'

'Oh c'mon, let me pay, it doesn't matter.'

'That's what I'm saying... it doesn't matter... so let me.'

'Oh, we'll keep talking like this and the shopkeeper will keep seeing us like this' I said drawing Shikha's attention to the vendor. The vendor's expression suddenly changed from an irritated face to a shallow smile. 'And it doesn't look particularly good for a girl to pay if there's a person like me around.'

'You sure?'

'What's there to be sure about? Next time you'll pay, deal done' I said and cleared the fact that the next time we were meeting it was her pockets which needed to be full; I had acted smartly, hadn't I?

'Great to spend some time with you, dear lady' I said coming out of the shop. 'When are we meeting next?'

'You say; I'm always ready' Shikha said and maybe this was what didn't irritate me hanging out with her. She was not like the other girls who will take hundred hours of persuasion to be taken out. Those are the ones whom I address as the *non-deserving girlfriends.*

'Okay, I'll call you when I get time. We'll decide over the telephone' I said getting close to Shikha for a goodbye hug... it was probably more than that... the same chill ran through my veins just as it had done on the day of Shikha's birthday...

On my return journey back home, I mused over a matter- believe it or not, at last I had found a *girlfriend* for me...

Oh, don't laugh... it's not that easy... in a nation like ours', we have to work very hard to get a girl out for a date... especially when you have at least five other boys battling for the same girl... who knows how many boys would be wanting to spend sometime with Shikha but I was the fortunate one- I was *actually* getting to spend time with her...

Also, I want you all to be aware of one more fact, and I'm telling it because I'm really loyal to all my readers (I ought to show some respect to the people who dared to pick this book which belongs to a debut writer)... *your parents would have said- 'oh gosh! At least buy some book of a renowned author, who the hell is he?'* No, they didn't speak like this... then you have not bought this tome... I feel dumped...

So, getting back to the fact, I must admit it's only people like me for whom girlfriends are scarce; if you are the hunk of your school, there are chances you might not face such paucity... but to be the hunk, you need to be smart, you need to be the school football team's captain, you need to play an electric guitar... and there are some other criteria that are required to be fulfilled but the above listed ones are primary...

Just one more thing- you remember Shikha had asked me to think of a name for her, and I hadn't thought any. I was glad that Shikha didn't put out that topic during the date, because if she had, I wouldn't have been able to come up with a good answer.

Enough, we've discussed much about girlfriends; now it's time for the second night to approach and I waited for it desperately... particularly when the first-night stay was such a success- it made me comprehend things which I would have never appreciated otherwise... let's see what the second-night has to offer...

# 12

# Second Night, More Bright

Sleeping was the first thing I subsided to as soon as I reached home after my short meeting with Shikha. And I had to doze, because I knew tonight was again going to sleepless; I couldn't imagine resting at Pranav's home until Zayed was around. But only after a night-stay I had realized that it was for good- he had given me nothing less than a worthwhile experience which I could treasure for the rest of my life.

More importantly, it was tonight that Raj and I had planned of watching some Hindi horror movies and maybe some English ones-the only requirement being that they contained some *scenes* for us to savour. Raj had informed me that he would be reaching my home at about nine, after taking some DVDs from Pappu. You haven't forgotten him, have you? Yeah, right-Pappu was the one we all turned to for a variety of reasons.

Talking about Pappu, I would like to share a feeling of mine with you. Even if you don't like, you have no other option than to read it. Here is where my supremacy lies... sorry, I'm superior in no ways... just got a bit carried away...

So, Pappu is the center of my topic here. As you are already aware of, the plot of this book is real and thus there does exist a *Pappu* in my locality. You know what; even the name of this character is real. I thought of changing it to something more *elite-type* but just then guessed the original name would suit better... so I kept *Pappu*...

I had never expected Raj to be on time and there were no reasons why I should have. He was half-an-hour late today and that didn't bother me very much, but something else did- he had not brought DVDs which were his part of the plan to make our stay interesting.

'Hi, late again?' I said as I haphazardly looked for my slippers underneath my bed.

'Yeah, mummy again didn't serve me on time.'

'Fuck you. Get grown up boy, you ought to make your dinner yourself by now' I teased.

'Ah ha, as if you make it yourself? And anyways, I've more important things to do' Raj said.

'You self-short people, you haggard, mummies are not made for just serving you day and night' I said.

'Maybe, but I don't think so. After all, everyone has their own role to play in the family and they need to abide by it.'

'Oh, and are you playing your role?'

'No, not totally.'

'Then you should' I said and was surprised that I was advising my friend to do something that I was very far from.

'Okay *master sahib*, will you please shut up?'

'Sure son. Show me which DVDs you have brought?' I asked suddenly remembering about those.

Raj looked up at me and then again kept his head down. This merely meant that he had not only come late, he had not brought the DVDs either.

'Boy, you have not taken the movies?'

'Nope' he said blankly.

'Total jackass, that's what you are. Damn, now we have to go and take the movies also. Raj, you know what- you don't simplify things, you intensify them further' I said.

'Oh, I knew it, thanks anyway. Now be fast or else Pappu will close his shop.'

'Thanks for the information; I thought Pappu remains open 24x7'.

******

The shop wasn't very far from my place and so it didn't take us much time to reach their by my bicycle. Pappu's shop was flooded as always; with people who had no work other than discussing what's going in and around the locality lately.

'*-they took all the gold from the house, and also told them to keep tight-lipped in front of the police-*' I heard one of them say.

'*-yeah, they also harassed their daughter*' the other one quickly let go of his precious knowledge.

At the end of the day, you might have recognized that Pappu's shop was one in which all the hooligans of the colony gathered at this time to discuss matters of *premier* importance. But I don't want you to make out that the shop was a large one, rather it was diminutive, so minute that only the owner could remain inside it. Pappu as ever was one of the most imperative individual in giving his opinion on such issues.

But we only knew the other side of him; he was welcoming, friendly and sociable to us and this was the major reason that all we friends went along so well with him. Resultantly, he was a buddy of all- of the hoodlums and of us.

'Raj, Arjun, coming at this time?' he spotted the two of as we made our way amongst some people to face him.

'Yeah... what's the time? It's not even ten' Raj said.

'No it isn't, but it still is a strange time for you to drop in' Pappu said.

'You want us to leave or what?' I joked.

'Of course not, what do you want, any movie?' Pappu asked as he signaled the other people in the queue to wait; oh, he was showing us some importance, or maybe he wanted us to get away from there sooner rather than later.

'W-we want some Hindi h-horror m-movies' Raj was feeling embarrassed to speak this out but he had to.

'What? Hindi horror movies?' Pappu was astounded.

'Yeah, you don't have those?' I asked.

'I've everything, Arjun. More than what could you be on your wish list. But tell me- from when have you all developed a liking for Hindi horror movies?' Pappu wasn't still ready to believe that we were *actually* asking for them.

'Why, I heard they are good' Raj said.

'Oh, did you? They aren't horror, they'll make you laugh' Pappu said.

'That's what we want, and be quick, we don't have much time' I notified.

'Sure, select whichever you want' said Pappu as he brought us a carton full of what-we-were-wanting (really, Pappu was a well-equipped man).

After about five minutes of vigorous search, Raj and I arrived at a common decision- we selected a Hindi horror movie which I'm sure even its makers would have forgotten the name of.

'This one,' Raj said, 'we'll take this one.'

'Okay, you can pay later. You want anything else?' Pappu asked and he was always like this; he didn't worry much about whether we paid him or not.

'Right, tomorrow, you'll get your twenty bucks. Just show us some English movies, something *r-romantic*, you understand?' I asked.

'Yeah, take these, all of them are new' Pappu said and handed us some DVDs. It didn't take us long to select this time; we picked up a movie which looked absolutely sensuous by its cover; surely we didn't have any idea about the cast. In fact, pictures like these were the ones which attracted us the most.

'Right, off we go' Raj said as he showed Pappu the DVD he had taken.

'Fine, see yaa. Good night' said Pappu.

'Good night' Raj and I said together.

*****

Again, Zayed was already there when we arrived at Pranav's home and he asked the same question as he had done on the previous day- 'Late again? Aunty took time in serving you dinner, eh?'

'Yeah, what else' I said.

'C'mon, as if we didn't have to take the movies' Raj said.

'What movies?' Pranav said as we seated us comfortably once again on the vast bed that covered most of the room's interior.

'Oh, forgot to tell you both, Raj and I took some movies for us to see' I updated the situation.

'Great, you both are not very big fools as your faces' suggest' Zayed said.

'What did you take?' Pranav asked.

'Fuck you Zayed,' said Raj, 'we are so smart, aren't we?' Raj shrugged showing Pranav the movies we had chosen.

'Of course you are, but what is this that you have taken?' Pranav was surprised at our selection of the Hindi horror.

'Yeah, that would be lovely, we'll surely enjoy watching it' I said.

'This, huh? I doubt it' Zayed said analyzing the cover. 'The other one will be perfect, I feel.'

'Both of them will be great', Raj said. 'And I guess we'll watch them after midnight, eh?'

'Yeah, of course, we would be awake all night; hanging out yesterday didn't prove out to be a problem, right?'

'No, except for the math teacher leaving the classroom' Pranav said.

What was to follow was a series of questions that Raj and Zayed kept on banging and Pranav kept on answering. After the narration of the morning incident was over, Zayed concluded that his friend had done the right thing by forcing the teacher out of the class.

'Oh gosh, I didn't force him,' Pranav said, 'I hadn't done anything which ought to deter his mood.'

'He sucks' I said.

'Yeah, he does. And what was worse- Pranav even apologized to him, after which he moved out, strange' Raj said.

'Good, at least we get a moral from all this' Zayed said.

'What?'

'That we shouldn't apologize for anything until we are wrong' Zayed justified.

'Absolutely, forget it' I said as my phone vibrated (I had forgotten to turn off the vibration mode after the tuitions). It was a message from Ravi, and a real exquisite one. In fact, it was so good that I ought to share it with all of you. It went something like this:

*Life of a 12$^{th}$ class guy:*
*Computer hai, net nahi*
*Kapde hai, pressed nahi*
*Wallet hai, cash nahi*
*Lecture hai, attendance nahi*
*Mobile hai, balance nahi*
*Bike hai, petrol nahi*
*Friends hai, girlfriend nahi*
*Exam hai, tension nahi*
*Padhna hai, mood nahi...*

'This is awesome,' Zayed said as he finished reading it aloud, 'great analysis. It matches us perfectly.'

'Yeah, except for one thing- I don't even have a bike, I've an old rugged scooter' Raj complained.

'Superb, it depicts our life in such a simple way' Pranav said. 'We could put it in big black letters on a white canvas in front of our school and proudly say- SEE, THIS IS OUR LIFE!'

'Good idea, only the school won't allow' said Zayed with the same childish smile he had every time after he said something *funny*; funny according to him. In reality, he was one of the worst joke-crackers I've ever met.

The next fifteen minutes passed with the four of us discussing about how fast SMS' had become an important means of communication.

'It does the work of a pager' Raj said.

'Yeah, mobiles have developed a lot in a last few years; I remember my uncle possessing a one-kilo mobile set which he was very pompous of,' Zayed said, 'he used to proudly say-*this cost me sixteen-thousand rupees.'*

'Right, it's not only that they keep developing, the manufacturing cost keeps on decreasing as well' Pranav presented his perception.

It was about half-past ten when Zayed spoke out his hidden wish of the moment. Strangely, it wasn't about making us do push-ups all night.

'I want to have some ice-cream' he said.

'W-what? It's surprising' Pranav said.

'The idea of having ice-cream at this time?' Zayed asked.

'No, not that, but the fact that our thoughts match so much; I was also wanting to go out for some ice-cream' Pranav said.

'Going out, at this time?'

'Yeah, Maurya Complex would be open and it's not far either' Raj said.

'And we have a bike and a scooter as well' Pranav said.

'I have only twenty bucks in my pocket, which will do, eh?' I asked.

'No problems, I've the money' Pranav said.

'C'mon, let's move then' Zayed said.

The bike belonged to Zayed's father and he only gave it to his son so that he could reach Pranav's place quickly. He wouldn't have known that Zayed was using it to carry his friends at eleven in the night to an ice-cream vendor.

I didn't know how to ride the scooter, nor the bike. My father possessed a *Zen* which I knew to drive. So, Zayed started the motorcycle and Pranav started the scooter; oops, the only exception being that it didn't *start*!

'What the hell?' Pranav seemed livid after three unsuccessful attempts to turn the ignition on. 'This scooter sucks.'

'What happened?' Zayed asked who had already taken out the bike for the journey ahead.

'Dunno... though I guess it'll not start now, so idea dropped' Pranav said.

'No ways,' Zayed said unable to imagine his idea of eating ice-cream getting choked, 'let me try.'

He tried everything he knew but the scooter failed to respond. I guess it had no effect on me; I had eaten too many ice-creams in the last one week.

'I can't go there walking' Raj said.

'Nor can I' I said laying my hands on the scooter as well; who knows when these machines could act in response.

After about every attempt was made with no accomplishment, Zayed forwarded his proposal.

'We still have the bike though; I can load all of us' he said.

'Are you crazy, four people on one bike?' I asked though I had already enjoyed that kind of a ride once; I was careful not to mention that experience here.

'Why not, I've no problems' Zayed said.

'Okay, we can go then' Pranav said.

'It'll be very congested' I let them know.

'Doesn't matter, it's too small a distance and we won't have any checking at this time either' Pranav said.

'Okay, be fast, the vendors are not just waiting for us to arrive' Raj said.

'Right' I said.

The plan of a small trip wasn't such a bad idea after all. Zayed had absolutely no problems in riding the bike on roads which were mostly empty except for some people walking down the alleyway. Since Pranav belonged to this area of the town, he equipped Zayed with the knowledge of some short-cuts. It took us about ten minutes to reach the place which had seven ice-cream hawkers lined in a row.

Zayed stopped the vehicle near an old vendor and asked us the flavours we desired. I was bored of eating every one of them and so overlooked his offer.

'Which one will you take?' Zayed shrugged.

'None, I have just had them in the evening' I said.

'C'mon, take anything; you should appreciate Zayed's efforts' Pranav said.

'Okay, an orange lollypop will do' I said.

'Sure?'

'Huh, what's there to be sure about?' I asked.

'It feels so independent; I feel on top of the world now' Raj said.

'Exactly, we've no one stopping us from what we want; we are the bosses' Pranav said.

'Yeah, this is rocking, you want to be awake, don't sleep. You want to go out for some ice-cream, no problems. Get anything you want,' Zayed was flowing in emotions, 'Pranav, I want to thank uncle for giving us such an opportunity, uncle rocks!'

'You are talking like a drunken man' I said.

'I'm actually *drunk*' Zayed said.

'W-what?' This wasn't for us to believe.

'Really, I'm *drunk*' Zayed said.

'What are you talking about, don't joke' Pranav said.

'Okay, did I say I've drunk rum or vodka or something? I took coffee before coming to your place' Zayed said gesturing towards Pranav.

'Fuck you, you moron,' Pranav said 'I believed you.'

'And what made you believe me?' Zayed asked.

'Your personality I guess' I said. 'Right, Pranav?'

'Yep, your personality' Pranav said licking his ice-cream from all possible sides.

'They are right. If somebody would say Pranav drinks, I'll slap him but if somebody says that you drink' said Raj to Zayed, 'I might believe him.'

'What? But I don't drink' Zayed said.

'Oh gosh! We know that, for god sake, please give this huge dude some brains to think' I said extending my hands towards heavens, 'Raj intends to say that your persona is different, you are quite like the hunk.'

'Oh, I don't think so. Not a girl comes behind me,' Zayed said, 'you look at Pranav- he is the one girls always turn to, not to a jackass like me.'

'You really are a jackass,' Raj said, 'have you ever tried yourself in between girls? Have you ever got time from your *post-school duels*?'

'Dunno... let's talk about it at home. It's getting late' Zayed said and kick-started the bike.

With his extra-swift drive, Zayed didn't make us feel any pains during our trip back home. It took merely as much time as it takes a debut batsman to celebrate his maiden ton in cricket.

Once we were home, we quietly proceeded to the bedroom where we were supposed to sit down comfortably and carry on the conversation we had dropped midway. It was probably the most hushed ten minutes in the time we had spent at Pranav's home since yesterday... or maybe not... it was more quiet when we had waited for the *blackmailer's* call last night... dunno... I can't decide... maybe you can...

'So tell me what were you asking?' Zayed asked as we finally assembled on the divan.

'You were answering rather' Raj reminded.

'Oh, I was saying, if you think I'm the hunk, hunk according to you all, why is that girls are attracted to Pranav?' Zayed asked. I felt Pranav was trying to increase his level of attentiveness in the discussion.

'Pranav is a *girl-adorable* kind of a dude, hope you don't mind' I addressed the subject.

'Are you mad? We are friends, man, how the hell do you expect me to mind matters like these? Speak freely; I've every right to know what my pals think about me?' Pranav cleared my doubts by speaking these words.

'So-'

'-wait, I want to say something' Raj said.

'Yeah, please.'

'Zayed, we didn't say that you *are* the hunk; it's only that I feel that you are a raw material. You have the *potential* to become the hunk' Raj said. 'But for that, you'll have to behave more like them, not only go and get involved in every second fight that takes place at school.'

'Yeah, you need to go in between the girls. Just as our very dear Pranav does' I said.

'What do I do?' Pranav retaliated.

'You do nothing, for heaven's sake, is my every friend such a dumb? I want Zayed to realize that he has the same potential as you have of attracting girls' I said.

'The only exception being that the girls engrossed by you both would be different-types' Raj said.

'Exactly, that's it. Raj is spot on, guys,' I said, 'let me make something very clear to you. May I?'

On seeing that everyone nodded as a symbol of their permission to let me speak my heart-out, I continued.

'Listen, there are two types of men to whom the girls get attracted to, and it's basically because girls make an impression about a guy in the initial stage itself. Fine, any problems till here?'

'No' Zayed and Pranav spoke in reflex. Raj, on the other hand, seemed to meticulously enjoy my brief lecture on the *possible-ways-to-magnetize-a-girl*.

'And those two types of people are- the first is the *caring-one type* and the second is the *masculine-type'* I said.

'I've a problem, sir' said Zayed raising his hand. Big achievement this was; really was... I had become professor at such a young age...

'What, son?' I asked in an enigmatic style.

'How do we classify between the *c-caring-one type* and the w-what... yes... *m-masculine-type*?' Zayed asked.

'I share the same problem, professor' Pranav said.

'Simple, the first one is a kind of a guy who is cute-looking, smart, and gives a girl *I'll-be-your-very-nice-friend* kind of an impression' I said.

'That's the *caring-one type*, right?' asked Raj.

'Yep, that is. We have a great example- Pranav.'

'W-what, I?

'Absolutely, don't tell me this isn't the attitude of yours' that girls adore, apart from you being exceedingly soothing to their eyes' I said.

'Yeah, I agree' Raj said.

'And what's the *masculine-type*, then?' Pranav asked.

'That's the one we were talking about. One who doesn't give a damn to girls, but mind you, only from outside,' I said, 'from inside they want every beautiful girl to be their chum.'

'Huh, that's too complex to understand' Zayed said.

'They are the ones,' I continued ignoring Zayed's difficulty, 'who are big, muscular dudes. Men who could do seventy push-ups without letting an "if" from their mouths.'

'Great, Arjun, you have understood every bit of it' Raj said.

'There is no other option mate when you aren't either of the two,' I said dourly. 'You have no other option than to analyze the reasons that the girls get fascinated by a dude.'

'You have any example for the second type of guy you mentioned?' Zayed was desperate to know whether he fell into any of the categories.

'There are many examples, though I'm not able to recall a single one of them now. But you are the second-type of the dude in the making,' I said to Zayed, 'provided you don't mess it all up.'

'Me, are you nuts?' Zayed was overly under-confident.

'That's your problem. Change your attitude man; you can take some tips from Pranav for that matter' Raj said.

'Right. Zayed, you need to start noticing girls if you want them to notice you. You'll have to start right now, then only you can be among the top hunks in your college' I said.

'Yes, I think Arjun is right,' Pranav said referring to Zayed, 'you really are the raw material. You have the shape, the height and of course the charisma.'

'Precisely, you see, now even the *caring-type* dude has understood it' I said with the broadest grin that could have found place on my round face.

'Right Zayed, go for it' Raj said. 'And please bring some confidence in yourself in affairs related to girls.'

'Alright, I'll try; it's more difficult than tackling three boys at a time.'

'And please get yourself off these fights,' I said, 'hunks only brawl when required.'

'Yeah… I understand' said Zayed sinking deep into some kind of thought.

'I think Zayed has got it' said Pranav. But there was something in the big dude's expression that made me feel he hadn't entirely grasped the concept.

'What man, any problems?' Raj asked.

'No… actually yes' Zayed said.

'Whoa! How could a guy like you be shy? C'mon, ask whatever you wish, I'm ready to explain the full theory again if you wish' I said.

'Noah, I don't think that's needed, it isn't?' Pranav's forehead's muscles twitched.

'No, the full thing is not needed,' said Zayed pondering hard and I was surprised at him being so somber (my theory was proving to be a *theory*). From what had started as a funny sermon, my tips were now being considered as a sincere means for *self-analysis*. 'Arjun, would you be happy if you were me?'

'W-what does that mean?'

'If you were me, would you be happier than you are now?' Zayed was getting rather ridiculous.

My answer was a simple one, though it had some complexity involved. I think all this quiz session was just a consequence of us not being able to complete our quota of the day's sleep. I didn't know what I was telling, and I don't know *how* I was telling…

'Zayed, there are two aspects to it' I said and Pranav was getting irritated to say the least but he didn't interrupt me just as a true friend wouldn't have.

'What two aspects?' Raj asked.

'If I were you, I would have been very happy for myself' I said.

'Thanks, that's what I wanted to know' Zayed was cheery.

'But there's something else- I wouldn't be happier if I were you to what I'm now.'

'What the hell? It's easier to understand modern physics, what are you saying?' Pranav asked.

'I knew you all won't understand, drop it' I said.

'No, please, carry on' Zayed pleaded.

'Okay speak' Pranav gave his consent.

'I'm just saying that I'm content for what I'm' I said. This line is sounding cheap, isn't it? Three *I'ms* dumped into one line. Sorry, I had no other option.

'If you told me that I could transform myself into you or even Tom Cruise for that matter, I wouldn't have' I said to Zayed.

'Yeah, I understand,' Raj said, 'you are saying that we should be pleased with what we are?'

'Of course, and that's the way we all should lead our lives' I said getting exceedingly theoretical. 'Life's not easy mate and we can make it tougher if we don't believe in ourselves.'

'Hmmm....'

'Having said that, Zayed,' I continued, 'I would be very pleased if I had a personality like yours' but that doesn't make you deduce that I'm not glad with what I possess.'

'Is that it?' Pranav asked.

'Yeah... I think so' I said letting out a deep breath.

'Then may I call David?' Pranav asked.

'What for?'

'I think the clock stroked twelve while you were busy in your *I-don't-know-what-discussion* and its David's birthday today.'

'Oh... yes, I had forgotten it totally, call him, quick' said Zayed reaching out for the phone himself.

'Helloooooooo' said David in a somnolent voice.

'HAPPY BIRTHDAY FATSO' Raj roared. He was so loud that there was no phone needed for his voice to reach the birthday boy's ears.

'Thanks, you all remember it.'

'Why fatso, how did you think we'll forget that?' Zayed asked.

'No, I didn't think that, I thought you all might be too busy enjoying the stay' David replied.

'Happy Birthday mate, hope you prosper even more, that doesn't mean that I've given you the consent of getting chubbier' Pranav said.

'Thanks, you moron.'

'Wish you many happy returns of the day, and I'm always ready to see you get flabby, okay cutie?' I wished.

'Thanks babes' said David. 'You all are coming to the party tomorrow, right?'

'Tomorrow, huh? You'll give the party one day after your birthday?' Raj asked. 'I mean today is your birthday and so the party should be today as well.'

'You, total dim-witted, tomorrow means *today*' said David. 'You all are coming, eh?'

'Yeah... of course dude... how can we afford to miss that?' Zayed said.

'Noah, you can't... we'll meet at Pranav's place after tuitions tomorrow, okay?'

'Of course, this surely is the ideal meeting place' said Raj and I wondered how right he was. Pranav's place was the real juncture for all of us to congregate.

'Great, hope to see yaa all at eight tomorrow, good night' David wanted to end the call (anybody would do that who has to go to school the next day except Zayed).

'Good night,' said Raj, 'let's rock tomorrow.'

'Sure, bye.'

'Bye.'

******

Tonight was different from yesterday. Unlike yesterday, we were not feeling drowsy tonight. Probably it was because of the fact that we were mentally prepared; we knew we had to be awake all night. Though we were not sure of what could be done for passing time efficiently, we involved ourselves in some or the other activity.

It was about one in the morning when Pranav unveiled a surprise that he had kept in store for us.

'I thought hard, and then came up with the idea of playing a game tonight' he informed.

'What game?'

'Okay wait, I'm coming in a jiffy.'

I had never imagined that Pranav would have thought of a game like this- he had brought four half-liter bottles each of which contained some colourless liquid in it.

'What are these for?' I asked unable to figure out anything.

'Any guesses?' Pranav said.

'Dunno... not for sticking into the asses, eh?'

'No dumbo, you know what is inside these?'

'Yeah... those are soda bottles I guess,' Zayed said, 'I've never seen this company label though.'

'Right, I couldn't get a better label near my home at eight in the night, just bought them before you arrived, Zayed' Pranav said.

'Okay, but will you tell us what do you intend of doing by these?' Raj said.

'Yeah... there are four bottles as you can see and we are four of us here-'

'-so' I interrupted.

Pranav was never to the point. Will anyone please tell me what was the use of informing us that there were four bottles? Sure, we've eyes and we could spot them and if we could spot the ten-inched bottles, surely we could spot ourselves (I think our heights exceeded ten inches).

'Let me finish,' Pranav continued, 'so as I was saying there are four bottles containing half-liter soda each. We'll have a competition; all of us will take a bottle each and start gulping the fluid, whoever finishes first will be crowned the champion.'

'Huh? You know how tough that's going to be?' I was practical.

'Yeah... I know... going to be tough but it's going to be exciting as well... we are staying together for doing things like *these*' Pranav said.

'Oh, and I thought we were together for some combined-study' Raj said.

'I think it's a great idea' Zayed said.

'What, the combined-study one?' Raj inquired.

'No duffer, the competition,' Zayed said, 'but what will the champion get?'

'Nothing, you are talking as if it's some official *soda-gulping* tournament' Pranav said.

'Noah, there should be something, and that too not only for the winner, but for the loser as well' Zayed was thinking hard.

'What do you mean?' I said.

'Okay, I've got an idea. The one who finishes last will have to do something that the other three want, something which would be within his limits of course, and the people who'll finish second and third will combine money for a treat to the victor, okay?' Zayed's notion was brilliant.

'That's unfair I think,' Pranav said, 'it's unfair to the one who finishes last.'

'By no ways it is', Zayed said. 'He'll not even have to pay for the champion's treat. And anyways, anyone who finishes last deserves this much at least.'

'But there's no difference between the second and the third finishers' Raj said.

'Of course there is, the third one will have to pay more for the champ's treat', Zayed said. 'Okay, what do you all say?'

'Thumbs up from me' said Raj at once.

'Hmmm... okay... thumbs up from me as well' I said after musing a bit over the *prize-distribution* scheme.

Pranav was still not ready and I think it was because of the fact that he doubted his ability to finish in the top three. He was seeing his plan of an exciting-game boomeranging.

'Okay Pranav, you agree?' Zayed said.

'Yeah... I think so but I still-'

'-where is the opener?' Zayed was really energized at the prospect.

'Yeah... here... take it' said Pranav handing the bottle opener to the big dude.

'I'll open all the bottles and keep them on the table; we'll all pick one each and start guzzling, okay?' Zayed was getting increasingly animated.

'Right.'

It took merely three seconds for Zayed to open all the bottles up and keep them on the table.

'Here, off we go...'

And on we did...

'Aaagghhhh... this is horrible' I said as soon as I neared the soda bottle to my mouth. I couldn't believe my eyes when I saw Zayed's bottle half-empty already.

Then I turned my eyes towards Pranav, and seeing that he was also in full stride, I started swigging the soda.

'Who-oh-oa... I'm the champion' snarled Zayed when I had not even completed a quarter of the content in my bottle. Really, this dude possessed all the qualities one needs to be the hunk, and I was happy to have him on my friends' list...

'W-what, h-how could you be so q-quick?' asked a desperate Pranav for some tip so that he didn't finish last.

'I didn't talk like you,' said Zayed, 'now be fast, or you'll be the loser.'

It took approximately a hundred and fifty seconds from this point for Raj to finish his bottle of soda and I could see clear signs of relief on his face. He would be better-off finishing second and giving Zayed a treat rather than finishing fourth and do something which the other three desired.

Realizing that I couldn't afford to finish last (who knows what would happen to the one who did), I increased my speed of the *soda-intake process*. This was cruel, it absolutely was... if you don't know how we felt, you could try this game with some your friends some time... and don't forget to keep a prize for the winner... that spices the spirit...

Now, only the two of us remained, and I had a feeling that we were going neck-to-neck...

'C'mon Pranav, c'mon,' cheered Raj, 'you can do it.'

Maybe Pranav was lagging, then only Raj thought of cheering him up but I was wrong, yet again...

'C'mon Arjun' I also needed it. You need the support of your friends in crisis-crunched times.

And that was it...

'Oh-wo-oh...' I had finished.

Then I saw Pranav- he had not yet completed...

'Aaagghhhh....' Pranav was reluctant to finish his quota, 'I feel like vomiting...'

'Oh, do you? Then get out of here, this is a holy place' said Raj. Yes, these were friends...

'Fuck you, it's just a phrase, I guess now I don't need to complete the bottle?' Pranav said.

'No, you have to' I said.

'But why, I'm over and done with last position anyway.'

'You need to; we've all finished ours' said Raj.

'What's the use, please have mercy' Pranav pleaded.

I think it was his compassionate face and *not-so-good-acting* that propelled us to have pity on him.

'Okay, you can do without it, but you'll have to do what we want' said Zayed.

'I've no other option.'

******

Wondering hard on what could be the best recompense for Pranav's wonderful feat of not being able to complete a half-liter soda bottle (that's the least expected from a student of class XII); we finally arrived at a decision. We had to make sure that not only the reward suited his *talents*, but also provided us some entertainment.

'Okay Pranav, ready for the job?' Zayed said.

'Yeah... I think so, hope you all remember that it's your friend that you are asking to do something.'

'Whoa! Don't try to emotionally blackmail us and anyways, we'll not ask you to commit a murder' said Raj.

'Oh thanks, I thought you might do' Pranav said.

'You have to dance' I said. We had thought of it using our brains, we were sure Pranav would just loathe to do it.

'W-what, I don't know how to' Pranav said.

'You are not dancing on *nach baliye,* so please be quick.'

'Please, I don't know a thing, ask for something else' Pranav was expectedly hesitant.

'Oh c'mon, get grown up, only friends are here, and your dance is not going to be telecasted on TV' said Raj.

'Are you sure?'

'Of course we are, now be fast, we've other things to do' said Zayed and with this Pranav was on the floor ready to show a glimpse of his just another aptitude.

'I'll remember this,' he said before commencing, 'I really will.'

'That's why we've asked you to do this' said Raj.

What followed could not be elucidated into words, and not because I'm a young writer and am unaware of the skills to define experiences, but because it was such a dance whose bliss could only be enjoyed by those who witnessed it... luckily enough I was there...

It was hilarious...

It was ridiculous...

It was unbelievable... unbelievable because there are people on this earth who dance like this...

One of the ugliest dances I had witnessed in my life, Pranav's art-form was one which might force even the professionals to quit their careers, but it was certainly one which made us laugh like wild animals ..

and you believed me? Have you ever seen wild animals laughing? C'mon, apply your brains...

'Okay, you happy?' asked a sluggish Pranav after he had completed a boogie which was side-splitting.

'Happy? That was uproarious,' said Raj, 'now I'll ask you to dance whenever I fail in any subject, it's a perfect laughter-therapy.'

'Oh, was it that bad?'

'Yeah... it was' I had to admit the truth.

'I hope I could have shot it with a video camera' said Zayed.

'No problems, it was such a live-wire that it'll be fresh in your mind till death' I said.

'See, I made the night mirthful, I deserve a treat as well' said Pranav.

'Yeah, you really do' said Raj still rolling on and off the bed.

******

There was nothing very significant that marked the second night other than us dropping to the idea of watching some movies. Realizing the fact that it wasn't providing us the pleasure we expected, we played another game-this one being less risky and more universal-truth and dare.

'Yeah Arjun, what do you choose, truth or dare?' asked Zayed.

'Hmmm...' I was unsure, 'dare.'

'I'll ask something easy from you- just do forty push-ups.'

'F-forty?'

'Yeah... are they less?'

'Fuck you... they are very much, I don't think I can do more than ten' I said fully conscious of my credentials.

'What man, such a shame' Pranav imitated.

'Oh, as if you could do more' I said.

'Start at least, and stop when you can't continue' Zayed said and this made my job easier. Now it was up to me; I could have terminated the *push-up procedure* anytime I wished.

'One... two... three...' they started counting.

'... ten...'

'Great man, you have crossed double figures' congratulated Raj and I think I deserved that. I had surpassed my own expectations... I was a bad judge...

'Fifteen... sixteen... seventeen...'

'Whoooof...' that was it for me.

'That's it?' said Zayed.

'Yeah... seventeen I did, right?' I was in high spirits on realizing the weight of my accomplishment.

'Okay, let's continue the game' said Pranav.

This time it was Zayed's turn.

'Truth or dare, Zayed?'

'Of course dare.'

'Okay, you have to do just seventy push-ups' I said knowing the capacity of the big man.

'I think it's a bit more... should be fifty' said Pranav.

'No, it's fine,' reassured Zayed, 'it really is fine.'

'... seventeen... twenty... thirty...'

'How do you do these so easily?' I was amazed but Zayed wasn't listening; he had full concentration on the completion of the task assigned to him.

'... fifty... sixty...'

'You are awesome man' said Raj.

'... seventy...' I announced.

'Do you want more?' asked Zayed as soon as he finished this exercise. This was unbelievable; how could a man who had just now concluded seventy push-ups ask for more?

'Do you practice these?' Pranav asked. We needed to know the hidden reason behind Zayed's excellent physique and fitness levels.

'No, where'll I get the time from?' Zayed said.

'You can do seventy push-ups anytime you want?' I was frenetic.

'No, I think I can do more than hundred' said Zayed.

'You've got it naturally then' commented Raj.

'Dunno... maybe my build allows me. Whatever, I'm happy for it.'

'Who wouldn't?'

Next came Raj's chance and he also chose dare. But because of the fact of us getting bored with making everyone do push-ups, we asked him for something else.

'You go to the terrace and spend ten minutes there' Zayed said.

'W-what... at this time?' Pranav didn't enjoy the idea.

'No problems... I'll love to' said Raj and jumped off the bed.

Since Pranav's place was not only small in curvature but also in height, one had to merely cover a flight of twenty steps to reach the terrace. And Raj being wildly happy at the prospect was up there in no time.

About five minutes after Raj's departure, he called us to join him.

'C'mon you guys,' his distant voice said, 'the breeze here is scintillating.'

I thought of the night, the gentle wind and the enjoyment that Raj might be going through at this time when it was usually scorching during the days. All these thoughts acted as propellers for me driving my way up to the set of steps.

'Where are you going?' Zayed asked.

'To the terrace I imagine' I said calmly.

'But you'll join him; I mean Raj is there because he chose dare.'

'He's having fun, and that's what I'm going to take pleasure in,' I said, 'you two also come, let's spend some time up there.'

'Okay, let's go' said Zayed and the remaining two of my friends joined me on my journey to the top of the house.

'Wow! It feels great, we should have been here early' I said on reaching the pinnacle of Pranav's place.

'Yeah... I told you... it feels like heaven on this time at the terrace' said Raj.

'You are talking as if you always visit the top of your house at half-past three in the morning' I said.

'Not always at half-past three,' said Raj, 'sometimes at four as well.'

'Huh?' this was surprising.

'Yeah... I go there when I don't feel sleepy.'

'C'mon, don't kid' Pranav said.

'What's there to be kidding, eh? Whenever I want to feel the effect of a serene and soothing night, I'm out there' Raj was blasé.

'And your parents allow?'

'Ha, as if I'm a two-year old kid.'

'Strange, I must admit most of the parents won't permit considering this habit as some kind of a malaise' Zayed said.

'Right, very true' I said.

'It's strange for me, it's amazing how different the lifestyles of two people can be and still they could be friends' Raj said.

'Yeah, friendship is not decided on parameters' said Pranav.

'That's our best invention,' I said, 'I wonder how much the meaning of it has changed in the current age.'

'True. Now people are even jealous of their pals, of people they say are their lives' said Zayed.

'But we are true friends,' said Pranav, 'eh?'

We were talking of *real* friendship and so I couldn't just drop in with an everyday answer- 'of course mate, we can *die* for each other.'

It was complex rather… so none of us said a word… Pranav, as if not able to appreciate the gravity of the situation, asked again.

'It takes time for you to decide we are friends or not? It's amazing' he said.

'It's not that easy' Zayed said.

'Then what are we, just classmates?'

'Maybe' Raj said.

'This is implausible; I thought we all were *true* friends, we know so much about each other' said Pranav.

'It's not just about that,' I finally said feeling the swift wind caress me on the cheeks, 'it's how much we care about each other in the long run. A true friend loves his friend more than himself, you understand?'

'Nope' said Pranav.

'Okay, may I ask you something?' said Raj signaling to Pranav.

'Yeah… what?'

'Please be honest Pranav; tell me when the last time you told a lie to any of us was?' Raj was serious.

Pranav didn't say anything…

'Please say, you think we all are friends. You need not say to whom or why you said that?'

'Hmmm... it was yesterday I think' Pranav said.

'Then we are not *true* friends till now,' said Raj, 'as simple as that.'

'But there are many things we don't disclose to even our parents, that doesn't mean we don't love them' protested Pranav.

'Right, but they are your parents, not friends' Zayed said.

'You want to say that all of us aren't *real* friends?' Pranav said.

'Time will tell,' Raj said, 'as for now, I just see another Raj in you guys and that's why I love spending time with you all.'

I was unsure whether this discussion on amity and aftereffects was going to be of any avail. But there was one thing for certain- maybe we didn't make any use of the three nights academically, but this stay was enough for me and my friends to realize how much importance there was for us to know what we actually *were*, and what we actually *wanted* to be.

We didn't stop here; we went deep into our futures and conversed whether we were living to our parents' expectations. A big NO emerged inside my little head...

This was our age to enjoy existence, to know what fantasies our short lives had to offer... on the other hand this was our age to study, our age to build a platform which could eventually lead us to our ambitions... this was not easy... finding a balance was not easy... probably because we were not allowed to find a balance...

'The education is system is flawed,' said Zayed at one point, 'here we've to think whether we'll be able to survive.'

'And all this IIT stuff, dump it' said Pranav.

'Yeah... very true,' I said, 'the brightest minds of the nation reach the IIT. And what does it do? It conditions them to a living in which those buffoons just see money day and night.'

'What do you want then? They produce a superlative batch of engineers every year' said Raj.

'To hell with the engineers,' I continued, 'they should produce intellects, they should produce scientists, they should produce people that the nation should be proud of possessing.'

'Exactly' said Zayed. 'There should be practicality in their approach. I think the students who are able to crack the entrance examination have enough raw in them to be polished and presented before the world.'

'You know what- IIT is not a good institute' I said.

'No, it's not like that. You can't say it isn't a good institute, it is held in such high esteem not in the country, but abroad' said Pranav.

'What is the work of a good educational institute?' I asked.

'What... dunno... you tell?'

'To turn a mediocre into an instigator,' I said, 'IIT does just the opposite; it turns an instigator to a mediocre.'

'You want to change the IIT or what?'

'We don't have that much capability, just the style of teaching needs to undergo a major revolution' said Zayed.

'Then why are you running behind the IIT yourself?' asked Pranav.

'I'm not and I've realized that coming to this school. The IIT is not for people like me, or rather I'm not a person for the IIT' I said with conviction.

'What, then what are you going to do?'

'There are many things, one just needs to explore' I said.

'But your parents, I mean they might have high expectations from you' said Raj.

'Of course they have, and I'm not disappointing them either. Just because I've opted myself out of one stream doesn't deter my participation in the other' I said.

'You need to be practical' said Raj.

'I'm *practical*; I told you I'm not made for the IIT.'

'That's negative attitude' said Pranav.

'No, in fact it's positive. I'm looking for better options' I said.

'But your parents,' Raj wasn't just leaving them, 'how'll they think when you tell them about your sudden change in idea?'

Here is where I had the upper hand. Believe it or not, my parents were probably the most understanding and I was sure they would welcome the modification in my approach. Anyways, they just wanted me to be a good citizen after all.

My father always said- *'There is nothing that I desire from you, it's only that I want you to be bold enough to face the world.'*

The finish to this night was a tantalizing one... and it was so because we started feeling sluggish with the break of daylight and we knew we had to go to the school yet again, the place we loathed the most...

I've been with you for a week now and I'm sure by this moment you might have known that I'm not the one which you could expect to conquer the world. I'm just another one of those guys... for whom studies are important, but life is too... for whom family is important, but career is too... for whom friends are important, but girls are too... I'm just another one of those guys...

Some people might have enjoyed my company, some would have found it dull... but there's one thing that I've- confidence... yep mate, I've confidence on myself... I don't care what others think... in my eyes my life is already a success...

Deviating away from my life and what it has provided me in a few years in which I've subsisted on earth, I need to move on to other things. Today again I had to go to the sucking place but there was always some respite- there was a party tonight followed by my last night-stay at Pranav's place... of course there were brighter things to look forward to...

# 13

# Terrible Tuesday

No, no, please don't... please don't go by the name of this chapter... don't think that the last day of the week that we've lived and enjoyed together (I doubt whether you've enjoyed, I most certainly have) has a sad climax... it doesn't... when anyone studies in a school like mine, every alternate day of his life has got to be terrible... it's just that I was searching for a word to give an alliterating effect... so I chose *terrible*...

However, on Tuesday I had another worthwhile experience at the end of the school which I won't like acknowledging again... you'll come to know about that as the day progresses...

It was tough... readying myself for the school was tough... both mentally and physically... I was feeling sleepy even after taking a long shower which I was most unused to... anyways by accumulating all my self-strength, I forwarded myself to the place we call school...

Though the *boring place* had little to offer, guys like me had always searched for reasons to somehow complete the required minimum attendance that the school demanded. Yes, the reason was girls... of course we wanted to meet our dudes, but we could meet them any time we wished... it were the girls for whom we had to go to the school.

I'll have to admit one thing though- our section had lesser number of girls compared to other sections, C, for instance. But we had something else which kept me high in moods.

'-I'm happy for that, we've more girls than your section,' said one of my mates who was in C, 'we're happier.'

I was quick to react- 'maybe that your section exceeds us in quantity, but our section excels in quality.' This was true, and then only we had formed the *beauties* group.

You remember the girl I had liked on my very first day in class XII? You remember her name? Yes, Surbhi... I've been involved so much with Shikha lately that it's not your fault if you've forgotten girls like Surbhi and Priya... err... you are less familiar with that... the *sexy waali* I must say...

Though there were other girls in my section who were worth watching, but it was something about Surbhi that kept me glued to her face the whole time I was in school. No, there was nothing phenomenal about her beauty; maybe it was the naïve expression that attracted me. And I was not the only one drawn to her; there were other guys who appreciated her splendor.

Since I had nothing else to do at school, I mentally compared the two girls- Shikha and Surbhi. Yes, it's true that I've no rights to draw differences between them since I had no idea about Surbhi character-wise but again my decision was not an authentic one, so there were no harms. I came up with a simple result, though Surbhi was the one I was attracted more to, it was Shikha in which I found a friend for me. She had been awesome... that's the word a boy will use who particularly hasn't been much with girls since childhood...

There would be some questions raised on why didn't I nominate Priya in this *evaluating-the-girls-course* and I've a good reason for that. I wasn't drawn temptingly to Priya (I wasn't drawn irresistibly to any girl as a matter of fact)... only I found her exceedingly sumptuous... and c'mon, I couldn't put the name of every girl I knew...

'How's Shikha doing?' Pranav asked me in the math period.

'W-what, S-shikha?' I was surprised at Pranav's sudden inquiry but tried to keep my voice calm, 's-she is doing just about f-fine.'

'I still can't guess the reason why you didn't talk about her to us' Pranav said.

'I told you,' I reassured, 'I've been with her only for a week.'

'And you've been going well with her?' he asked.

'Dunno... though I guess she enjoys my company' I was truthful.

'Really?'

'Yeah... I think she does' I said.

'Great'.

'I'm also comfortable in her company,' I continued and seeing a twitch in Pranav's eyebrows, quickly added, 'compared to the other girls.'

'Compared to the other girls? Ha, that's a joke. I assume she's the first girl you've been out with?'

'Yep... I'm not like you in matters related to girls. I'm not experienced like you, either. I feel experience helps, eh?' I said.

'Of course it does, you know exactly what to speak to make the girl in your vicinity happy' he said.

All this talking was going on when the math teacher was scribbling questions one after another on the blackboard. He had realized what kind of guys we were-*talkative backbenchers*. He had come to know that by now, and then only he had summoned us twice on the first bench already in a week. We were lucky today though, we had not caught his eyes as yet.

'You're right; I need to take some tips from you, despite the fact that I can handle one girl at a time' I said.

'What do you mean by *one-girl-at-a-time*? I don't take care of ten at one time either. I've only one girlfriend and that's Zeesha' said Pranav.

'Right, Zeesha is the one for you' I said wondering how loyal Pranav was. I was happy for him; he was concentrating entirely on Zeesha in spite of regular temptations offered by other girls. That would be the case with you if you are good-looking, so I suppose Pranav was no exception.

After a vital chat about girls, we changed the topic to David's birthday. We thought about what an appropriate gift would be (I'll have to admit-Pranav is not only good at selecting gifts for girls, he is good at doing the same for boys as well).

'A football will do, it suits our budget' said Pranav. Don't be surprised, we gave a combined gift to our pals on birthdays.

'Yeah... not only does it suit the budget, it'll be also fine to have one more football in our possession' I said.

'So deal done then- we're presenting a football to David on his seventeen... err I don't know which birthday' finalized Pranav.

We were aware of one more fact- that we had to involve ourselves in an incessant exchange on some or the other issue, for we could not afford to feel sleepy again today... Pranav didn't wish yesterday's scene to be repeated...

The school was as mind-numbing as always, except for a *rap* song that Kishore had made involving our English teacher and the principal. The theme was based on the former, with the latter providing *punches* at regular intervals of time.

'Awesome man,' I complemented, 'you should be a lyricist.'

'Yeah, not only that, you've made good use of our principal' said Pranav.

I realize that we've probably talked about every issue that marks the life of a teenager except for the fact that I've not informed you the knacks of our very dear principal. He was rubbish... an absolute crap... this school was such a numb place because of the presence of this nuisance creature... I'm fully aware that I shouldn't be using such harsh words for someone as big as him, but I can't stop... my frustration doesn't look likely to discontinue...

There are rumours that the principal was once a peon, and if you some day unfortunately get the pleasure of a tête-à-tête with him, you'll know that they were not wrong. He doesn't know how to manage a school one bit... I know it's not an easy job but this bad... goodness me... he was more engrossed in filling his boots than thinking about the students' welfare.

Forget it... just forget it... this country works like this. And one can't do much to change it. Just sitting in an air-conditioned room and discussing the nation's problems wouldn't do it any good. It's an easy job for me to take the weight off my feet and criticize the country for its failure but it's a total different ball game to try and work in a positive direction.

*'The police here sucks'* we say. Why don't you join it and change the system?

*'The politicians are selfish'* we say. Why don't you become an elected official and set a rare example?

*'The school is hell'* we say. Why don't you just forget about all the weaknesses and think of topping the school's result-list?

There is a simple reason for all of it- who would take so much pain? It's better to leave the nation as it is, and just get on with your bloody work. This nation is great... just some people have got corrupt... and I'm one of them... and maybe you are too...

I'm no patriot...

I'm no jingoist, I'm no loyalist, I'm no nationalist, I'm no partisan, and I'm no flag-waver... I'm just an average middle-class student striving to see my nation on top of the world... so it's not that I get dreamy, it's only that I speak my guts-out...

Getting to my *not-so-monotonous-daily-life* as I always do after a dialogue with you all, I must tell you why today was not the best day of my week. I had not come to the school by my bicycle, and so I had to hire an auto for returning home. Pranav and Raj both used to go back home by the same means of transport as the school authorities had started checking bus passes from this week onwards. Thus, it were those two, along with me, who proceeded to the place where auto-rickshaws were present in huge numbers for carrying us to any part of the town we desired.

Pranav and Raj both used to go back home by the same means of transport as the school authorities had started checking bus panes from this week onwards.

Thus, it were those two, along with me, who proceeded to the place where auto-rickshows were presence in huge numbers for carrying us to any part of the town wedesired.

'Boring Road roundabout,' said Raj, 'and there are three... err four of us.' Yes, there was one more dude with us who was supposedly our class-mate, but we didn't use to converse much to him apart from formal talking. He sat on the front with the owner of the auto and the remaining three of us occupied the back-seat comfortably.

Though I've said that this place was quite flooded with auto-rickshaws, but it wasn't entirely all the same. One had to be lucky for getting four seats on an auto for the same destination and I think we were lucky... or maybe we weren't...

'I think this auto was made for us' Raj had said on spotting the empty vehicle with unwarranted glee making his face look self-indulgent.

'Yes, good we got it for where we wanted' I had replied.

The first impression that I got about the vehicle-driver was that he was young... by young I mean that he didn't seem to be highly experienced... and secondly that the vehicle was old... by old I mean it was over-experienced... but thinking that this was the way they used to be, I didn't bother about the matter any further...

'You'll be coming to my home or should I ask David to pick you?' asked Pranav from me.

'I think it would be good if David drops to my place on the way through. Or maybe I'll be coming directly from tuitions. In any case, I'll let you know' I said as I saw the driver grip the handle very hard, as if trying to stop it from venturing on its own.

‘Okay, that would be no problems, which restaurant would you prefer?’

‘Dunno… David’s choice’ I said.

‘David said he would take us anywhere we want to, of course taking account of his budget’ said Raj.

‘I think *Kaveri* would be fine, I’ve been there before’ said Pranav.

‘Yeah, I’ve been too, it’s reasonable’ notified Raj.

‘Ri-’

‘-oh… gosh’

‘-no…’

‘Whaaaaaaaaaaaaaam…..’

The next thing I found myself doing was following Raj out of the auto. He ran at least ten meters away from the place where the accident had taken place… Pranav was coming towards us clutching the thumb of his right hand very firmly… showing the mishap had a physical upshot on him…

Nothing much had happened… our auto had crashed straight into a bike standing on a traffic signal and in turn the bike had brutishly hit a car further in front… the next scene we witnessed was the bike owner gaining consciousness and reaching immediately for the auto-driver… poor auto-driver…

Our classmate who was accompanying the vehicle-owner was out of our sight at once, maybe he was hurt… sure he would have been… the auto had turned an angle of thirty degree from the back; it was an unpredicted calamity…

We were lucky that the accident didn’t hold a physical bearing on any of us, apart from a mere convulse in Pranav’s thumb but it was exceedingly minor… minor when you consider the injury that the auto-driver had suffered… his right leg was broken…

'You bastard, I'll kill you' said the biker who had been hit and he punched right on the face of the already half-dead auto-driver.

'Please sir, have mercy' pleaded the small man.

'How dare you ask for mercy? You must be beaten to death' said the biker accompanying his thoughts with a bang on the small man's head with his helmet.

I couldn't see all this... this was inconceivable... a man who had already suffered a major injury was being hit with such vindictiveness... true, it was his fault to have struck the bike which was stranded, but where was the humanity? And nobody dared to speak a word... all were mere spectators... and so was I...

'I feel gutted,' I said, 'absolutely gutted. I can't do a thing to save the small man.'

'Oh, this is sans humanity. He's being beaten so badly. Oh gosh, I can't stand this' said Raj.

'Should we go and give him the fare?' asked Pranav.

'I don't have the guts to give him money while he's being all messed up by the mob, I can't do a thing' said Raj.

'We're helpless man; let's move on from here, I can't bear this' I sighed gesturing my two friends to leave the situation as it was.

We acted like cowards... and we couldn't have done anything more... what could we've done? Asked the biker not to beat the small man? Who knows he could have blessed us too with a touch of his hand... the horde here has herd-mentality... instead of stopping the man from beating the hell out of another, they *clap* and *praise* as if enjoying a wrestling match... I was glad at least we weren't like them... if we couldn't help the small man from getting flattened all ends up; we weren't helping the biker in his process either...

'Had you been the biker, would you have done the same thing?' asked Raj as we forwarded our steps towards our homes.

'Couldn't dream of,' I said, 'maybe just rebuked him a bit.'

'Yeah, that should've been it,' said Pranav, 'and now they'll ask him for money. Where on earth will he get that from?'

'Dunno... why everyone in this world isn't like us?' said Raj.

'Yeah... it would've been such a nice place to live in' I said. 'We don't want anybody being hurt, do we?'

'Nope, and we are happy to see others happy. When will this world change?' growled Raj to the heavens.

'Now that's a tough question, only a philosopher can answer this, not ordinary men like us' I said.

'I imagine this is the first time any of us have experienced anything like this?' asked Pranav.

'Yeah... first time for me, and I don't want to experience it again, it was horrific' said Raj.

'It was man, and the worst part is we couldn't do anything to change it' I said.

'Yes man, we're no heroes like they show in the films who can handle all this in a jiffy' said Pranav.

'Yeah... they look good in films, in real life, all of that is crap,' I said, 'I think it's first time in my life that I'm unhappy for what I'm.'

'Exactly, I feel the same, but I think it's no good discussing it. The fact remains that we were vulnerable, and thinking more about that will only deteriorate us in our eyes' said Pranav.

'Yes, truth never changes. Forget it' I said.

'Yeah... that's the easiest way out' said Raj.

'Right, hopefully we're in a better position next time around.'

******

I didn't forget to share the day's misfortune with my coaching mates and they looked at it with the same prospective as I had; none of them seemed cherished on knowing how shoddily the auto-driver was treated.

'Yeah, but you should've tried to give him the fare' said Karan.

'Are you nuts? In the middle of everything, who would dare to?' said Ravi.

'That's the problem, everyone is afraid' said the huge dude.

'It's easier told than done,' said Vicky, 'I'm sure you wouldn't have dared to give him the fare either.'

'Dunno... maybe you'll think I'm boasting, but I would have tried to' said Karan.

'-stop it; I'm noticing you all talking continuously from the last two minutes' howled our chemistry teacher.

'-sir, it wasn't me, it were the other guys who were chatting' said Jai who had the teacher's gaze transfixed on him.

'That's what our nation's mechanism is,' said a relatively unruffled educator, *'either claim or blame.'*

'Oh, beauty...'

'-lovely...'

'-true sir, very true...'

And there was a sudden uproar from all of us; we applauded on the teacher's meticulous observation. I think we clapped more than what the America's populace had done on Vivekanand's lecture on *zero*... or something similar...

'Isn't that right?' said the teacher jovial with the applause. 'I think it suitably fits the scenario.'

'It does, sir' said Karan looking merrier than the teacher on diversion from the topic of *haloalkanes*.

'Sir, you rock,' said Vicky unable to control his feelings from pouring out, 'you are simply the best.' And he was spot on; we loved this teacher because of the interaction he had with all us, he was like a friend... and moreover he knew his subject more than the other teachers in the town did.

'Now that's emotional blackmailing' said the educator.

'It isn't sir,' I said, 'our teachers at the school suck.'

'Bad manners Arjun, they are your teachers after all.'

'To hell with teachers, they don't know what they... err... *know*' said Vicky.

'-for heaven's sake, please stop...' growled sir, but he was never angry, never furious even when we forced him to... in spite of regular enticements from our side, he even chastised us with a touch of love...

Have I told you anything about his age? I realize I haven't... any guesses from your side? I think you are imagining him to be cool and dynamic, somewhere in his thirties but I must say that you're wrong, and that too badly... I'm happy that I'm not the only one to give out bad judgments... on the contrary, he's in his late fifties, and he shares our mindset...

Our coaching continued till quarter to eight and Ravi along with me rushed to Pranav's home after that. Yes, Ravi was invited too. And on the way through, he gave me significant, or rather good news.

'I'm staying tonight too' he said serenely.

'G-great, that's wonderful' I reacted.

'Yeah… Pranav asked me if I could stay, and I asked uncle, and he allowed' he said.

'Let's make this night worth remembering,' I said, 'today we're five of us there.'

'By the way, where are we leaving from Pranav's place?'

'*Kaveri*, I suppose.'

All the friends were already waiting at Pranav's home which we popularly called the *junction*. On spotting the birthday boy, I bashed into him.

'HAPPY BIRTHDAY' I said with a wild hug, a hug which would have made the twenty-five kilo overweight David striving for free air.

'Oh, thanks, thanks a lot dude' he said.

'Happy birthday man,' said Ravi in his *Shahrukh-style*.

'Thanks man, I've seen you after quite some days' said David.

You don't know much about Ravi and it's my fault; I haven't been much with him; actually the plot didn't allow me to make him a regular customer, though that doesn't mean that he isn't one of my closest friends.

There are very few people in this world that could be like him- an absolute winner in his own rights. He is always everyone's prey; there isn't a person in the school who knows him and doesn't make a mockery of his personality. But he is generous… he just smiles and laughs… he is happy when others laugh… even when they laugh on him…

*'How could you be like that?'* I had asked him once, *'if somebody would've done that to me, I would've either beaten him like hell or wouldn't come to school.'*

*'You know what Arjun, nobody intends bad, they just want to have some fun, what's the harm if I provide them that?'* he had replied.

*'You are awesome man'* I had said.

*'Ha, that's what you think, nobody else does.'*

Yes, Ravi was the subject for anyone who wanted to create some comedy; not only that, he himself was great at creating atmosphere. He had a tiny crush for Pranav's girlfriend and he admitted that without a stint of hesitation in his voice.

*'Zeesha is incredible, super cool,'* he used to say to Pranav, *'just praise me in front of her. Praise me so much that she finally dumps for me.'*

*'Not possible dude,'* the other pals said, *'not possible considering your face.'*

*'What's in the face man? Today I'm Ravi, tomorrow I might be Shahrukh.'*

He perfectly knew that he wasn't good-looking... but he also knew he possessed great temperament... and that's the reason he hoped that beautiful girls will someday fall for him...

Now, let's overturn the time-machine... back to present...

'It's half-past eight here already' said Zayed. 'It would take one hour in buying a gift, and then probably another one in the celebrations. Mummy would kill me if I'm late.'

'Huh? What are you saying? You are staying, right?' Pranav asked in disbelief.

'Oh, actually no. Parents didn't allow, you see, and I can't defy their orders' said Zayed.

'But it's just one more day... err.... night' said Raj.

'I know... but you how Mummy is? She didn't allow, and I'm helpless' said the big dude. It was ironical to see him *helpless;* somebody who could fight with five boys at a time, and he couldn't question his mom's orders, couldn't dare to.

'Aaahhh, only three of us tonight' said Raj.

'Noah,' I said, 'today Shahrukh is staying with us.'

'Oh, really?' Pranav looked cheerful again.

'Yeah... uncle allowed' said Ravi.

'Fantastic,' said Raj, 'it would have been great if you stayed too, Zayed, but I'm happy that at least Ravi has joined us.'

'Great, you can enjoy even without me,' said Zayed, 'as for now, let's get out.'

'We are directly going to Kaveri, eh?' asked David.

'No, first we've to buy your present' I said.

'You could give that to me later. I want to be quick, actually papa told me to be back soon' said David.

'But it's your birthday today, you should get it today' Raj said.

'Please, for heaven's sake, try to understand. Give me the gift tomorrow if you wish. And it would also save Zayed some time' said David.

'Hmmm... I think fatso is right' Zayed agreed.

'David, can't you stay?' I asked fully aware of what the answer was going to be.

'Are you crazy? Papa wouldn't allow in his dreams, so please let's move now' David cleared the doubt It was comical; one of the either parents was the boss- in the case of Zayed, it was his mom and in the case of David, it was his dad with whom the supremacy lied.

It took nominal time for the six of us to reach the proposed restaurant. We had three scooters (Pranav had repaired his one) and so we sped in the maximum pace that the scooters could possibly have.

*Kaveri* was beautiful from inside; the perfect place to take your girlfriend out for a date. The walls were embroidered with ancient carvings that depicted nothing but romance, and passion. From the ceilings hung the flickering yellowish lights enough for one to scan through the food menu. The waiters here were classy as well- their outfit consisted of a red *kurta* and woven white *pajamas.* On their heads were long turbans which trailed their part till the spine.

There were two chambers each consisting of six seats on either side of the hall, and spotting one of them empty, we hastened towards it. Also, the chambers were set on a platform rising above the floor, so we had full authority of celebrating our friend's birthday in the style we preferred.

'This place is cool,' said David, 'quite secluded.'

'Yeah, just for families who want to have dinner inaudibly-'

'-and for friends like us' completed Raj.

The dim light didn't allow us to see each other's faces, though it was enough to make out their silhouettes respectively. The lights were quite different from the hall outside; fluorescent bulbs emitting contradicting colours were present at each corner.

'So what'll you all take?' asked David.

'Hmmm... let's see... butter chicken would be good' said Zayed. 'What say, guys?'

'Yeah... and we should take some tofu, it's the specialty here' I said.

'Right then, they'd be fine with *naan*, I wonder' said Pranav.

'Exactly,' said Ravi, 'right combination.'

It took about twenty minutes for the dinner to arrive. I guess they took more time than the other hotels; but we were ready to compromise- since they served better food.

'Here sir' said the waiter lining the plates on the table. 'I hope you love the food. Anything more desired, sir?'

'Nope, at least not for now, we'll let you know' said David with great authenticity in his voice as he was never addressed with such respect other than the member of staff serving at table. We always used to call him *fatso* or *wompy pompy.*

'Right sir' said the waiter disappearing behind a vaulted archway that stood at one side of the foyer.

'You talk about this' said David piercing through a leg-piece with his canines.

'Yeah... and this as well' I said gulping the biggest tofu bit present on my already multicoloured plate. I was never elegant at eating in hotels; I was like a villager at tackling situations like these... I was happy that we were enjoying our dinner in a separate antechamber.

'Why Shahrukh, how do you like the food?' said Raj.

'Oh, yeah... fine... not better than the *Taj*, I must admit.'

'Ah ha, sorry Shahrukh, we haven't been there. You are the star, you would've been to the best hotels worldwide?' said Raj.

'Yeah... many people invite if you are someone as big as me,' cackled Ravi, 'though the best one was the Grand Hyatt in Dubai.'

'So what's the plan for tonight?' asked David.

'Huh... no values for my experience' Ravi murmured to himself.

'Dunno... today we're not doing much talking, that's almost a certainty without Zayed' said Pranav.

'Why, am I a chat-box?'

'Nope,' I said, 'he means that we've various topics to discuss when you're around. Maybe we can finish seeing the Hindi horror tonight, it looked good at the beginning yesterday.'

'Good idea. And I'm feeling a bit weary, so I'm not going to school tomorrow' said Raj.

'Nor are any of us, especially after attending the *boring place* for two continuous days preceded by sleepless nights' I said.

'It feels so good when you know that you are free tomorrow, right?' questioned Pranav.

'Of course, you don't have tensions to bear' said Zayed. 'But fatso, thanks for giving us such a treat.'

'Why, have you completed?'

'Nope, a *naan* is left, can't I thank in between?'

'Oh, never mind. It has been a pleasure hanging out with you all' jeered David. 'Thanks for coming, all of you.'

'No problems mate, anytime you wish' said Ravi.

While everyone had almost completed the last portion of their respective *naans,* Pranav and I were struck in the second.

'I think I'll not be able to finish even two' Pranav murmured.

'Ah, nor will I' I said in a low voice. 'I'm amazed how my consumption level has decreased so much; I think it's your company which has such aftereffects.'

'Oh, is it? Or is it because you think a bit too much about the lady... yeah, Shikha?' Pranav taunted.

'Guys,' I announced ignoring his comments, 'I've had enough, I think I can't take any more.'

Pranav, happy to see me already proclaim, added- 'Yeah, I've had enough as well.'

'What, now I know why you can't do more than sixteen push-ups' said Zayed.

'Nope, it was seventeen' Raj corrected and started the previous night's narrative in his typical style that included periodic knocks of laughter.

'But what are we going to the food which is left, are you two sure you'll be unable to complete your quota?' asked David. Pranav and I nodded almost instantaneously in response.

'We can get it packed' Zayed gave his opinion.

'But for whom, are you going to take it home with you?' joked David.

'Fatso, your brain is also fat. We can give it to a beggar, there are so many of them sleeping around the roundabout at this time' said Zayed.

'Yeah, perfect idea,' I said, 'we can at least do something for the God to give us his blessings.'

Today we didn't have ice-creams as desserts; instead all of us chose our favourite sweets correspondingly. Pranav and I rejected David's offer- our stomachs were already full with excess food.

We sang loudly coming out of the hotel as if we were drunk, and none of the pals hesitated; they perfectly knew we were enjoying without disturbing anyone else. Not everyday was like this- we had the full authority to celebrate David's birthday in a unique way.

'HAPPY BIRTHDAY... DAVID... HAPPY BIRTHDAY TO YOU... MAY THE FOOD... ERR... GOOD GOD BLESS YOU' we chorused in a tune which even the best music composer in the country would have been proud of creating.

'-stop, there's a man there' said Zayed on spotting a vagabond whom I thought would have been in his late seventies at the first impression. On getting closer, I realized that he would be at least twenty years younger. He had a long beard trailing its way past his prominent ribs till the abdomen, with black and white colours being the chief ingredient of his ruffled tresses.

'Baba, take this' said Zayed handing him the packed food.

The old man was surprised; he couldn't believe somebody would offer him the food of the hotel in front of which he used to spend the endless nights. Then, gradually, his eyes showed content and a sense of happiness gleamed through his face.

'Thank you son,' he said, 'God bless you.'

I think I saw tears in their *eyes*; yes, tears were sheltered in the eyes of both the old man and that of Zayed- he had surely got emotional, he was always like that... a bit touchy...

'Man, you got emotional' I said to Zayed as he approached us after doing a fine job.

'Yeah... they are just in such pitiful conditions' he said. 'I wonder why god has left them in such precarious situations.'

'God knows' said Pranav.

'Right... only he knows' said Zayed signaling David and Raj to bring on the scooters. Now we had to travel the journey back to the *junction...* to Pranav's home.

It was an awesome small trip back home... we crooned songs all the way back. Though many people cast us *boorish-boys-of-rich-parents* kind of looks, we didn't mind them as we were lost in our own world...

*'Be a rebel... masti ki pathshaala... be a rebel...'*

There were so many times hitherto during the three nights that it felt as if we had a complete vodka bottle poured down our throats, but that was not the case even once. We were so absorbed in enjoying the stay that we were beyond our normal selves for most of the time.

*'-masti ki pathshaala... be a rebel...'*

'Life's rocking man' growled Zayed reaching the speed limits that the scooter could hardly provide.

'HAPPY BIRTHDAY... WOMPY POMPY...' we bellowed.

Though Pranav's place was not very far from *Kaveri* employing a couple of shortcuts, the trip was just a bit longer since we had paced ourselves in the normal route.

'THANKS DUDE, I'LL REMEMBER THIS FOR THE REST OF MY LIFE' roared David trying hard to keep in touch with Zayed.

I had never experienced anything like this before; these were probably some of the finest moments of my life. I had forgotten that these two years were most cruel for me academically, that I was not shaping up a bright future for myself... that I studied at a place I absolutely loathed...

'-see, they are drunk...' wheezed a short and plump man under his breath as Zayed raced the scooter past him.

My reflex forced me to turn my head backwards and act in response. 'We're drunk- and that too of stolen money; hope it wasn't yours' I rumbled. I saw the man casting a nasty look before we turned a sharp left and he was lost somewhere in the obscurity.

'This is insanity,' said Pranav as his scooter got close to ours'. 'But I love it, fabulous mate.'

'-yeah, this is paramount fun' I said as Zayed accelerated the scooter yet again as if a nitro booster was fit into it, he just couldn't let the poor vehicle move at an average speed.

Then, almost instantly, I don't know what occurred to him, he brought the scooter to a halt so abruptly that I fell forwards but the huge body of Zayed was always there to comfort me.

'Wait a minute,' he said and rushed towards a small grocery shop whose owner was out already to close the shutter.

Raj caught up with us easily enough and he was confused to see me stranded like this on middle of the road. 'Why are you here, and where's Zayed?'

'There…' I said pointing towards the small shop in which Zayed was in a conversation with the owner.

'Blimey, what took him there?' Pranav said who had told Raj to bring his motor vehicle to a standstill as well.

Zayed came rushing with two half-liter cola bottles towards us and it was strange for me to find out that he was not intending to drink those.

'C'mon, fast,' he said giving Pranav and me a bottle each. 'Splash it on David as he comes. Raj, you round David from the right and I'll do that from the left. Fast, start your engine, hide the bottles-' he broke off as David approached us.

'What are you doing here? I thought you'd be home by now' he said.

'We could have, but that didn't seem to be an appropriate idea without the birthday boy' Zayed said. 'Let's get going.'

As planned, David was allowed to ride his scooter at the middle of the road with Raj and Zayed covering him up from either side. Pranav and I were ready with the bottles.

'-off you go' bawled Zayed.

It was with immense difficulty that we aimed for David from moving scooters, but Pranav and I had succeeded in the job- we had managed to splatter all the cola on David narrowly missing Ravi who swerved quickly comprehending our intentions within seconds. 'HAPPY BIRTHDAY FATSO…'

The next moment, David was all drenched in black liquid though it only appeared colourless on his dark clothes. It took him a moment or two to realize what we had just done- 'you morons, I'll not leave you…'

'This is your birthday, wompy pompy' said Raj justifying our act.

'Yeah, we ought to have done something for you to remember the day' I said.

And again we chorused together for the last time in the night:

'WISH YOU A GREAT BIRTHDAY FATSO... HOPE YOU GET PLUMPER SONS...'

We reached our destination at about twelve and Zayed was not ready to believe that time had ticked by so quickly.

'Oh God,' he said nervously looking at his wrist watch, 'now mummy is surely going to *kill* me.'

'Don't worry, just tell her that we got a little late with the celebrations, I'm certain that she'd understand' Raj said.

'Hope so', said Zayed. 'Just give me a glass of water, I'll have to rush.'

Pranav hastened towards the kitchen as David was also getting a bit tentative. 'I'm wondering why papa has not rung me up as yet.'

'He knows it's your birthday, he'll give you at least this much of freedom' said Ravi.

'Yeah... you're right' said David. 'But you all are *real* idiots; you wasted a liter of cola.'

'We didn't *waste* it; we had much more fun seeing you get soaked up in the icy cold liquid' Zayed defended his idea.

'Yeah... here's your water, wished you had stayed too' said Pranav as he came up with the water which Zayed gulped in one take.

'Oh, would have loved to, but please try and understand. Tomorrow, nobody is going to school?'

'Nope, nor are you?' I confirmed.

'Noah, by no means, see yaa all, great party' Zayed said finally giving David a deep hug.

We all followed the procedure as we saw David and Zayed leaving the scene as a final point.

'Bye mate, good night, thanks for all of it' said David as he kick-started his scooter.

'Bye, and sweet dreams' we all said together.

******

This night might not be the greatest of the three in terms of us knowing more about each other, but it was good at something else- it was the first time I had laughed so much. The Hindi horror had proved to be much better than our expectations; we were amused that a movie containing such a baseless story could be approved for a release.

We snorted like mad men wouldn't have in the depth of night, rolling from one bed to another, and back to the first. It took us more time than an average movie would have taken; we paused at times vigilantly noting each and every expression that the actors made. One of them kept removing his spectacles and putting it back as a symbol of grief caused due to his brother's death; yeah, his brother had been consumed by a witch.

It was ridiculous and that's why I'm sharing it with you. Believe me, had you been there, you would've found my words true. Nothing in this world can make you guffaw and cackle for three continuous hours at the same rate as it had- I would've loved to give you a VCD of the movie for yourself to see and judge but I couldn't; some things are beyond my control.

'This- this is oh, boy, this is unbelievable' hooted Raj as he fell off the bed on watching a scene which he categorized as best of the lot.

'Yeah... great you brought this... ha, oh Lord, save me' screeched Ravi as he followed the scenes with surfeit concentration.

It was about half-past two in the morning that Pranav and I inhabited the owner's room while Raj and Ravi were still laughing voraciously in the adjacent room. As you already know, these rooms were separated by a door which was ajar now.

'Brilliant, how did you do that?' I was amazed at Pranav's superlative skill in a computer game.

'Yeah... just got to practice, only the third time I've done it though' he replied coldly.

'Still playing games?' Ravi said from the other room.

'Yep... got nothing else to do' I said.

And then Raj and Ravi started humming; humming so loudly that it overshadowed the violent music of the videogame.

They started with a recent Bollywood song which sounded even worse in their voices. It was a mixture of cheapness and tetchiness but we couldn't stop them; they had every right of enjoying in the way they found fit. Then, without notice, they changed the song to an English one. Though Raj remembered the lyrics well, Ravi faced troubles going along with the track; it didn't stop him from droning- he kept saying dissimilar words at times.

'Ah, I'm done, you try' said Pranav as he completed another level of the electronic game.

'Let's see, I can't play like you' I said pressing buttons on Pranav's keyboard haphazardly.

'What're you doing?'

'Ah, this- warm up' I said.

'Ha,' he smirked, 'but they are singing real bad, mate.'

'Oh yes, awful singing, one has to say,' I muttered. 'But Ravi thinks he's good enough for creating a music album of his own.'

'Oh, you can't blame him, can you? With the kind of music created these days, anyone who wants to sing just goes and squeals; you just ought to have enough money for summoning a famous model ready to strip off her clothes for the video. And the public loves it; no one cares what the hell they're singing, or wailing rather' Pranav gave the whole bureau of how the industry worked.

'I'm impressed,' I said admiring his observation, 'my company has started to show its effects.'

Our other two friends were still going on with the songs; now only they had changed from the baritone to a composition which sounded absolutely new- because it was there own stupid creation.

*'We love you Zeesha, we love you Zeesha, we love you Zeeshaaaaa... C'mon and give me a kiss, mere paas aa aa aaaaaaa....'*

'They're awesome' Pranav remarked. 'I just love them.'

But the song-originators didn't stop her, they just carried on...

*'Fuck you Zeesha, fuck you Zeesha, fuck you Zeesha...'* this time only Raj's voice echoed.

'No, no man,' said Ravi, 'remove the "fuck" word mate. Loving is okay, fucking is just a bit too harsh, don't you think?'

I thought I would see Pranav livid with bloodshot eyes wanting to cause some destruction, but he reacted in just the opposite way. He was rolling; he was expressing amusement by chortling in a high-pitched laughter.

'Man, they're too good,' he said, 'blessed to have got friends like them, I really am.'

'Are you serious?'

'Oh, what? Of course I'm. They're kidding man, don't say that you took it seriously' said Pranav astonishment clearly visible in his eyes.

'No- no I didn't, but just thought she's your girlfriend-'

'-she *is* my girlfriend.'

'Right, she is,' I was lost for words, 'I might not be that pleased if I were you.'

'Dunno... your choice mate. I don't mind that,' Pranav said firmly. 'Because I know they're just joking, having some fun, that's it.'

Pranav was speaking a bit too loudly and that made our friends think that there was some kind of a heated argument going on.

'You both fine?' said Raj entering the room. He saw from Pranav to me and then back to Pranav.

'Any problem?' asked Ravi who had joined too. He exchanged amused looks with Raj unable to make out anything.

'Yeah... everything's fine' I reassured. 'Just talking about how Shikha might be the right girl for me.'

Pranav's jaws dropped... even I was shocked... what was I speaking? How did I think of Shikha at this time? Maybe Pranav was right; maybe I was thinking a bit too much about her these days.

'Oh, then how is Shikha the right girl for you?' asked Ravi.

'R-right, she's the s-same k-kind,' said Pranav, 'Arjun told she loves sports too, and he could talk to her about f-football anytime he wished.'

'Blimey...'

'Interesting theory man,' said Raj, 'it's highly ridiculous though.'

'Yeah... that's what I told him,' Pranav teased me, 'but he told he'd like spending his life with a girl who talks about football rather than one who just desires romance.'

'Ha, it' amazing... you should spare the girls at least' shrugged Ravi.

******

Pranav went off to sleep after this conversation and a bit about the girl whom Ravi was concentrating nowadays. Raj, Ravi and I remained awake doing activities, which, I'm sure Pranav would have regretted missing.

It was about four in the morning when the three of us moved into the backyard and Ravi and Raj tried to copy a dance step which they had just seen in the movie tonight. They failed horribly, falling over each other, but it was loads of fun.

Though Raj was also feeling sleepy by the end of this procedure but he didn't sleep; he didn't want to make the only night Ravi stayed with us boring. So, instead, we cracked many jokes marking tonight as the *laughter-night*. We carried the process till about the time when sun rose brightly over the hedges of Pranav's home, bringing an end to a pleasurable, or rather fantasying three-night stay at my friend's home.

Maybe, or surely, there are some things that I've missed in this book; certain experiences that couldn't be given the face of words. I don't think anyone else could have shared them with you either, because they can only be felt by you yourself. So, I, with most honesty, request you to make a plan of camping out with your friends. And, believe me, you'll not regret it. Maybe you would understand the very essence of the force that propelled me to share my experiences with you.

There's one more thing which remains to be told- when I first thought of converting my life to a book which you could all live, I had considered of ending up here. But then something else happened with me at school, and I couldn't dare to miss that. It would make you realize, why truly, my school-life was hysterical had I not got such fantastic friends... and also, why our principle was such a numb living-creature... had somebody else been the headmaster, I might not have passed my exams with the name of this school on my admit card... I'll tell you why...

# 14

# Almost Expelled

Though I haven't had many good experiences of the *boring place* during the eighteen months I've been studying here, this was probably the most unpleasant of all. It was about two-weeks after the reopening of the school subsequent to the summer vacations (which I enjoyed like heaven) that this incident took place.

The summer vacations was like a blessing in disguise, we loved it like anything... while most of the IIT aspirants spent it licking their books, I made it pleasurable from the outset. There were football matches every alternate day in the morning, and we went to the field more than just to play. Actually, the state under-19 girls' team practiced that time, and we relaxed our eyes gazing on them. When the ball drifted its way to them, all of us ran at once to retrieve it. Yeah, the girls weren't mesmerizing, but we had no option... the school was shut...

Though I didn't get to see any of the girls of the *beauties* group during the vacation, I kept going on well with Shikha. She was getting intimately close to me by this time, but we had full control on our actions. We spent hours staring at each other's eyes, for no reason;

maybe I think doing that decreased the power of my spectacles... amazing, isn't it? I've spent so much time with you, and it's now that you know that glasses were a part of my personality...

Also, during this fabulous little stint, we kept remembering the gratification that we had gone through during the time which we had stayed at Pranav's place. About how much we had known about each other, about how much we had loved each other's company, about the push-ups, about the birthday celebrations, about how much we had laughed, about how much we had learnt...

It was a day before our return to the school that Pranav expressed his extreme undesirability to rejoin the place we loathed most.

'Noah, such a great time we had off it,' he said, 'I don't want to go back.'

'Who does?'

'Yeah, probably no one, there is only one reason that I feel cherished about' Pranav said.

'About meeting Zeesha?' I said the obvious.

'Yep... it's been a long time since I saw her.'

'Right... how do you spend so much time without meeting even once?'

'You know- she's not like... maybe someone like Shikha, for instance. And we keep talking on the phone-'

'What do you mean- *not someone like Shikha*?' I frowned.

'Oh, you understood otherwise. I mean she resides very far off, and you know how her dad is- doesn't allow her much time out' Pranav said.

'And how the ruddy hell you suppose me to know that?'

'Then you ought to' he said. 'You should know about your friend's girlfriend.'

'Ah, maybe, so everyone's coming to school tomorrow?'

'Yeah... I think so, though Ravi has not yet returned, so he's off.'

Ravi pounced on the slightest of opportunities he got of visiting his home, his parents. And I don't blame him; it's rather tough spending the life without them. But then, I thought, career was important, and it was for it that he was studying here away from his home, to fabricate a future for himself...

Returning to school wasn't much fun, and seeing most of the girls absent on the first day after reopening, it was worse. However, getting on with pals whom we couldn't meet during the vacations seemed to be the sole respite.

The weeks that followed were dull, without any kind of seventh heaven occupying our brains. It was about fifteen days after our return, when the unexpected occurred.

It was a blistery morning with small dark clouds hovering over our heads, and more number of students had come to the school than ever before. I mean that there were very few absentees. Our own class was flooded with students but I didn't mind that as long as every member of the *beauties* group was present.

It was a better day than the normal was at this place, with all of us cracking jokes as none of the teachers seemed in the mood of teaching. It had started to rain by the third period, and it had got darker outside. The lights went off, and we were told there was nothing that could be done to improve the situation as the generator had developed some kind of an infection within itself.

Our English teacher entered with his usual glum-looking face made worse with marks of ferocity lining his cheeks; it seemed as though he had just had a spat with one of the teachers. Yeah, this place was odd. Here, instead of the teachers cooperating among themselves to yield the best of students, fought among themselves for stamping their authority. And, our principal ignored this; all this was done right under his nose.

I, however, do not mean that our English teacher *did* have a duel with someone; in fact he was one of the few teachers at this place who was far off from incidents like these.

'Have you brought your books?' he addressed the class.

'No sir, not yet available in the market, and anyways the light is too dim for you to teach' said one of the boys.

'I do not need your suggestion,' the teacher spat, 'you could do whatever you like but don't disturb the other classes.'

We were more than happy at hearing this; only sometimes were the teachers here so generous. I was thinking this was going to be the best day after the vacations, but I was horribly mistaken.

I saw Kishore reading something very close to his face, not to mention his face was deeply drowned on his desk.

'What's that?' I asked.

'You want it, I've read it' he said. He was sitting in front of us and as always, Pranav and I were occupying the very last bench.

'But what's it?' Pranav also got interested.

'Yeah... all of us have read, fabulous, it really is' said Kishore. 'Vicky, Ashu-'

'But what the hell is it?' I was getting irritated. And I think I spoke a little too loudly; the teacher gestured me to keep my mouth shut.

'Oh, this- magazine' Kishore finally answered.

'Which one?' I said.

'Dunno... someone from the other class gave it.'

'But there would be the name on the cover' said Pranav.

'I'm not that foolish, these are only torn pages' he said showing that he had some three crushed pages in his hands.

'Show them' I said.

And Kishore handed them at once. Pranav bent to have a better look, and he looked amused.

'Oi, this is nude,' he said, 'but looks interesting.'

On the pages were a couple of pictures of bikini-clad woman in sensuous poses looking awfully inviting. And then there were some articles related to models' life and how they keep their figures opulent. Also, there were some things printed in multicoloured ink that one might not dare to read at school. But, knowing that we were sitting on the last bench and seeing the master not strolling, we began reading.

'Fine,' I said, 'interesting things told, eh?'

'Yeah, looking cool' said Pranav as we united our heads to look at the articles more closely. We had half-read the thing when I saw up to see the face of our teacher bearing thunders on our faces. Pranav tried to hide the pages but to no avail.

'What's that?' asked the master.

'N-nothing, j-just, n-nothing s-sir.'

'I asked to show that to me' the teacher growled and the students who weren't looking at us by this point turned their heads to see what had made the teacher to snarl like that.

My stomach lurched; there was nothing we could do… the hairs on my hand stood up, and my heart started to race, pump harder than ever. I was sure Pranav was feeling just the same… he handed over the pages to the teacher…

Our English teacher went through the torn pages, half amused and half disgruntled. Once he had found out what we were reading, he looked at us with interrogating eyes. He again went through the pages as if not able to believe that we were reading *this.*

'What's this?' he rumbled shaking the glasses of the windowpanes.

'S-sir, w-we don't know.'

'You don't know, you say you don't know?' he was trembling with rage. 'It is found in your possession, and you say you don't know.'

'S-sir, actually-'

'-get out, get out of the class.'

'Sir,' Pranav started, 'it was laying on the floor. It doesn't belong to us-' but he stopped midway as he saw the principal on the door. This was frantic; apparently the principal was strolling in the corridors and he had come to see what was it that was making our teacher shout like this.

For a moment I was stupefied. I didn't know where I was, or what had happened… then I regained my consciousness and heard Pranav whisper in my ears. 'We're busted man, we're gone. Hell, why had it to be us?'

'Come to the headmaster,' said the educator, this time in a much calmer voice.

I stood up and began to proceed to the door where the head of the school was still positioned, who was not able to make out one bit.

Then I turned back to see Pranav still sitting, not able to make up his mind. I also caught a glimpse of my other friends; their eyes were wide with fear, their face sunken with shock.

'I thought I asked you to come too' shrugged the teacher and this time Pranav stood up, with panic clearly making his face not appear as handsome as it usually was.

Our ten-step journey seemed to be a ten-kilometer one. I was thinking of excuses, of ways to escape. But nothing lit in my brain, quite empty brain at this time. As we approached the principal, the English teacher thrust the pages into his hand, and looked at us with pitiful eyes.

The worst was coming, it really was. After all, we had been caught reading a nude, or rather a porn magazine's pages in the high school premises. The principal analyzed the sheets, and wasn't able to make out anything.

'You boy, where is your tie?' he shouted at me, and I was taken aback. He was asking where my tie was didn't the hell he realize that we had been caught red-handed reading wicked things?

'And your wrist-buttons, why are they open?' he continued, and Pranav was as astonished as I was... the principal wasn't getting a part of it.

'S-sir, actually my tie is in the b-bag' I said with a better conviction.

'And you boy, why are your locks so long?' the principal now turned to Pranav. 'Call Dinesh, I should get them cut.'

The rumours were true then; our principal was a peon before acquiring this position. Here our future hanged in his sole hands, and he was busy in observing our uniforms and curls... he was thinking of summoning a barber named Dinesh for cutting Pranav's tresses... this was awful, yet laughable... he was being stupid...

And then, in a blur of action, the teacher turned the pages in our principal's hands. He seemed embarrassed, yet stuck to his purpose. Our principal's eyes, however, turned scarlet red, and it was now after seeing the bikini-clad women photos, that he understood the gravity of the situation.

'What the hell-'

'Sir, it's-'

'EXPELL THEM' the headmaster bellowed, as his body rocked with fury, his hands quivered with ire. 'THEY HAVE GOT TO BE EXPELLED.'

I hadn't expected this; yeah, I had thought of the principal summoning us to his office and then rebuke us as he hadn't done in days... but expulsion, this was unpredictable...

'Sir, please understand, it was laying-'

'WHATEVER, YOU HAVE GOT TO BE EXPELLED.'

'Please,' we begged, 'spare us, it isn't our fault.'

'Then whose, mine?' said the principal. 'Sir,' he turned to our English teacher, 'talk to their class teacher, who's it?'

'Das Sir' said Pranav. And it was with this answer that hope sprang back to my mind. Our class teacher was considerate, we could blackmail him emotionally.

'Right,' the heartless principal continued, 'meet him, and tell him to hand over the *letter of expulsion*.'

*Letter of expulsion... letter of expulsion?* We had to meet our class teacher before the English teacher met him; we had to explain him the circumstances.

'Could I trust you to get the work done?' asked the principal shallowly and the teacher nodded. With the answer he had expected from his junior colleague, the headmaster turned back and departed.

'Keep quiet,' the English teacher addressed the class, 'as you clearly see, these ill-mannered boys have been caught reading *immoral* things. They are going to be expelled, and if you don't want the same to happen with you, then keep quiet as I return in a jiffy.'

The teacher, Pranav and I left the class which was buzzing with thoughts; all the students seemed keen to discuss what lay ahead for us. But as we were leaving the classroom, I saw Kishore showing a thumbs-up and I replied with a flying kiss. You had to try and impress girls even if you are in dire states.

We proceeded to the staffroom which was at the end of the long corridor, and Pranav and I kept muttering our plans for the future. The teacher, leading the way, turned every now and then as if to check we had not run away.

He signaled us to stop at the entrance of the staffroom and entered the rectangular hall which was entirely visible as the door was left open. It was painted in brown unlike the classroom, which was of course painted in white. There were two closets in black placed adjacent to each other in the far-corner of the room. The wall on the other side was full of windows, allowing the air to sweep the insides of the hall. There were two long tables with several chairs assembled around each of them. On the farthest chair on the second table, sat our class teacher.

I saw the English teacher approach him, and then there was a long conversation in which I felt the former explaining the scenario. He also showed him the torn pages, making the slight hope inside my mind dwindle away. For once, I had thought that the principal had taken the pages with himself, for savouring them in his private antechamber. But he had returned them to the educator, for him to show it to the class teacher.

Then both the teachers proceeded towards the door where we stood in utter anxiety and fretfulness. Then our class teacher, who merely reached my chest, saw us with eyes that clearly approved that he hadn't enjoyed our act.

'You both will get the letters by the last period' he said.

'S-sir, p-please help, this is not ours'.'

'Sorry, nothing can be done. I assume you have got to be expelled if the principal desires so' he said tranquilly.

'Sir, I'm leaving, I've to return to the class' said the English teacher breaking in our discussion. I was glad that he had thought of leaving the scene; this action might have given us enough courage to plead forcefully to our class teacher.

'Sir, we don't want to be expelled' Pranav said once the English teacher had left.

'Who desires it, son?'

'We said it was laying on the floor' I raged in an undertone. Pranav pinched me just to remind that it wasn't the right way of talking.

'Sorry, it's you who has done the business. You need to pay for it' said the teacher and his casualness increased with every statement he spoke.

'P-please, our parents won't be able to take it' said Pranav. I hadn't thought of what my family's reaction would be until this point. My mother would be distraught. *'See, I always said he was going the wrong way'* I imagined her saying to my father.

Our teacher kept quiet.

'Sir, please try and *decrease* the detention' said Pranav.

'Detention?' said the teacher in downright bewilderment. 'What do mean by that? We are talking about your expulsion from the school.'

'Help us sir, please do.'

And then I didn't know what went through the teacher's mind that his tone changed. This time it was a lot huskier; maybe he remembered his days at the school.

'Okay, I'll talk to principal sir, you might be summoned. Just stick to what you've been saying so far- that it was laying on the floor and you were just checking what it was. Right?'

Words found it hard to come out from our mouth in reply to the class teacher's gracefulness. So we nodded our heads rather violently.

'Sir, what is the least that we could expect?' I asked.

'Suspension.'

'For how many days?'

'Till further notice is given to you but believe me, that's only a possibility. I hope you get away with that' the teacher said.

'I hope so... only suspension' whispered Pranav sneeringly.

'Will our parents be asked to come?' Pranav asked.

'Boys listen,' the teacher said, 'let me see what can happen in your case. And full details will be given to you in any case, suspension or expulsion. Now you ought to leave, I'll inform you.'

'Right sir' we said as we heard the bell ring for recess. Then we turned to proceed directly to the grounds, where I guessed a lot of pals would already be waiting to hear the full story.

'I think we've got away with it' I said as we descended the steps that led to the acres of free space behind the school building.

'Are you nuts? You remember what he said- *suspension is just a possibility*. And assuming that we get that, we'll have to still tell our parents. I think they would be in for bit of a shock' Pranav said.

'Yeah... shock either ways. It would be a bit more if they directly hear that their wards are expelled from the school on grounds for reading *immoral* parchments' I said.

It was beyond expectation. The story had spread like a wildfire across the school premises. A whole throng of students were interested in hearing our version of the tale, probably because they could connect with it in a better way.

'What next?'

'-getting busted?'

'-idiots, that's what you both are. Didn't see the teacher coming?'

'-what did Das say?'

'Suspension, that's the least to be expected. He'll try for it though' said Pranav.

'The problem is,' I said, 'this could probably be the worst reason for one to get deferment for. I mean, anything else could have been accepted at home, but this-'

'-talking as if we're sure about the action. HE SAID IT IS JUST A POSSIBILITY' Pranav broke off. He was looking pale; I hope Zeesha got a look on him now, she might've just realized that he isn't that handsome after all.

The lunch break passed with Pranav and me trying to answer the questions fired at us by our friends, class mates, and our own brains...

*How'd we tell our parents what we had been caught reading?*

*How'd they react?*

*What'd be the girls thinking about us?*

*Which school was best for us if we got expulsion?*

Not all, but some of the answers were answered with the end of the last period. Pranav had feared me with all kind off ill-thoughts that he could possibly imagine. His idea was that we had got expelled; that's why the principal didn't call us to his chamber, that it was the *letter of expulsion* that was being prepared; it was for its preparation that it was taking so long...

However, Das Sir had different notions. As soon as the bell marking dispersal rang, he came up to us and handled a letter each to Pranav and me.

'This,' he said, 'is your suspension letter. Don't attend the classes from tomorrow. And tell you parents or guardians to meet the undersigned, that to say is the principal. The sooner you tell them to meet, the better. I say that because I feel you'll be allowed to resume the school once your guardians set up a meeting with the principal personally.'

'Thank you, sir' we said and left the class with chain of thoughts surrounding our brains knocking a plan for the future.

And as I moved out of the gargantuan iron gates, I took out the letter sealed in a white envelope which bore the school's stamp on it. Then I opened the folded parchment to see what was doodled on it. The school's name was on the top with my name following closely. The letter was addressed to my father:

*Dear Sir,*

*I'm highly regretted to inform you that your ward is not following the disciplinary rules that our school has thrived for since the very start. Your ward was caught reading a morally wrong parchment during school hours which is certainly not what we expect from our students. His behaviour is jeopardizing the atmosphere of the class in particular and the school in general, adversely. The continuation of your ward's presence may prove to be an obstacle for the safe running of the school. We, therefore, abandon your ward from attending the classes and thereby, creating a detrimental ambiance for the students to dwell in. For the very same reason, we suspend your ward from attending the school till any further notification from our side.*

*You, or any person who could be considered a guardian for you ward, is requested to meet the undersigned in view of the very same. It's our job to lead the future of the nation in the right way.*

*Yours Sincerely,*

*Principal*

So, this was it: I was deteriorating the school's stature on the whole. How was I supposed to be an obstacle for the safe running of the school? Was I a terrorist caught planting a bomb in the school's premises? How could I be unhealthy for the school's esteemed environment by reading bloody torn papers of some magazine?

On one side where I felt an upsurge to *really* plant a bomb (provided that there were no students in the building, I won't mind the principal and a couple of teachers though); I also feared my nerve of showing the letter to my parents... there reactions could be unpredictable... I was especially afraid of my mother's. I didn't know how and when could I possess the guts to tell what had happened with me at the school, to inform my parents that I had been suspended for relishing nude photos, and papers in the English period. But then there was an answer, which I had not even thought of.

******

'Whoa! But I swear, I'll get you out of trouble' said Karan after the physics tuition that very evening.

'What? How could you possibly-'

'Yeah... I can,' he said proudly, 'fake parents.'

'W-what-? H-how-? *Fake* parents?' I couldn't digest this by any means.

'Right, I don't think you've too many options' said Karan.

'But what if I get caught?'

'Caught? I've full confidence in my actors. They'll give you a slap or two on your face if you insist... in the principal's office. That'd create the atmosphere?' said the huge dude.

'Noah, I think rebuking would do' I said.

'Are you crazy?' said Shubham for the first time. 'Karan is idiot, rubbish idea this is. You can end up busted.'

'As if I'm not already,' I defended Karan's plan, 'I've no options mate. We don't live in America, my parents wouldn't tolerate me being caught possessing some funny magazine's pages.'

'And will they tolerate when they come to know that their ward visited the principal with someone else, introducing him as the guardian?' Jai joined Shubham's idea.

Now it was a two-on-two battle...

'I said the actors would do fine, and honestly, your principal is the only one in town that could be fooled. Maybe it's a blessing in disguise, maybe your principal is such a dupe for a day like this' said Karan merrily.

'But I still don't think it's a good plan,' Jai said and added quickly as if struck with a brilliant notion, 'what about Pranav then?'

'I can arrange a guardian for him too.'

'Oh, really?' I was glad to hear that Karan not only intended to save me, but Pranav as well.

'Yes, you both tell the principal that they are your uncles, fine?' said Karan.

'Right, let's just go for it. Whatever beckons, I'm up for it. I'll be informing Pranav and other mates about this. When can your actors come?'

'Anytime you say?'

'Okay... how would be the day after tomorrow? Meanwhile, we can meet tomorrow to discuss the plan' I suggested.

'Okay, go for it' said Jai suddenly.

Shubham's stood there, astonished. 'Are you saying that, too?'

'C'mon dude,' said Jai, 'would be quite an adventure.'

'Okay, whatever you think fits' said Shubham patting me on the back. I was happy that everyone had agreed. It'd have been a hell lot difficult if any of my friends didn't approve the idea.

'Tomorrow, we are meeting then' said Karan. 'Bring Pranav too.'

'Of course I'll. We need to know who are guardians *are*' I said idiotically.

'Chinku... and Billoo... both fine' said Karan talking more to him, than to us.

'For god sake... Chinku? Billoo? Don't sound good by their names' said Jai.

'Believe me, they'd be excellent' reassured Karan.

'But Chinku?' said Shubham in disgust. 'You aren't bringing someone who gets them down, gutted?'

'No man, sometimes you ought to believe in the big bloke' said Karan referring to himself. 'Your stupid friend could be of some use.'

'I believe in you' I said firmly. I was already imagining Chinku, a small man, shorter than me in height and plumper, scolding me in the principal's cabin.

'Thanks.'

******

It was not as tough as I had thought. In fact, never are my predictions quite right. Chinku was a tall man with strikingly bright features, and he had a deep blemish on his forehead which he boasted he received in a fight with a policeman who had fired on him for not wearing a helmet. This, I thought, was boasting because he seemed to be the kind of person who would think thrice before dueling against a bunch of schoolboys.

On the other hand, Billoo was a relatively shorter man with as much fairness. His dressing sense was sophisticated to say the least; he wore a collarless striped shirt and a jute jacket which followed its way till his knees on the day when we met first to explain the roles. But one thing was certain- both Chinku and Billoo looked to be the right kind of persons for the job. Also, I had told Karan that we needn't introduce them as our parents; we could just tell the school authority that they were our guardians.

It didn't take Pranav and me long to decide our relatives. My dear friend asked me to choose whomever I wished as my uncle and I thought Billoo would be the one. So Pranav, very gleefully, accepted Chinku as his guardian. We explained the situation to them and also requested to reprimand us a bit in the principal's office if required.

The best part of the plan was that Billoo and Chinku didn't desire anything in return for their services. However, Karan had told me to give them a hefty treat once the job was successfully accomplished. Pranav and I, had, surely enough, agreed without the slightest of shilly-shallying.

On the day of action, all the four of us met near a temple which was not very far from our school. After the final bit of last-time rehearsals, all of us proceeded to the place which had changed my life completely in the last eighteen months. I keep talking about the influence of the *boring place* on my existence just to make you realize that it was after all, without much doubt, a *boring place* to prepare for your future.

We entered the school premises at about quarter to ten. There was a reason for choosing this time- our friends had their recess at half-past ten and I expected Pranav and myself to give out the news of our safe recovery from the disastrous event to them at that time.

But again, my plan went wrong horrifically. No man, don't think that principal recognized the real identity of the fake guardians; it's just that we couldn't meet our other friends.

The principal made us to wait till eleven, and it was highly disgusting; particularly when you know that the principal was doing this just to make our *guardians* feel that he had other important things to do.

At precisely five past eleven, the principal summoned Billoo and me to his office. Most certainly, by this time, my feet started to tremble. What if our plan wasn't successful? What if our guardians were robbed off their fake identities? What if our real parents were informed and we were issued permanent expulsion? Trying severely to wipe off these ill-thoughts, I filled in the form which asked for our purpose to meet the principal.

'May we come in, sir?' asked Billoo in a low-pitched rusty voice knocking at the glassy door of the principal's cabin.

'Yes... please do' said the principal looking up for a fraction of second who *seemed* busy scanning through some files.

The cabin was cooler, much cooler than the antechamber where we were made to wait for more than an hour. After all, there were two air conditioners fitted right behind the principal's desk.

'Please take you seats' said the principal pointing to the chairs in front of him separated by a table.

'Sir, I heard-' began Billoo but he suddenly broke off seeing the bemused look on the principal's face.

'Who are you?'

'I'm his guardian, Arjun's guardian.'

'Of course you are,' the principal said folding his hands and laying back comfortably on his chair. 'I mean what relation do you have with boy?'

'Oh, I'm his uncle.'

'His father's brother, are you.'

'No... actually his mother's. I think we are supposed to be addressed by the same word' said Billoo with great clarity. 'You can however add *maternal* as a prefix.'

'Maybe, do you know why you've been asked to meet me?' said the principal now seeming to place confidence on Billoo's individuality.

'Yes, I think Arjun was caught reading something?'

'Something? What do you say, something? There were bad photos in there, you shouldn't read them at this place' said the principal furiously.

'Right sir' said Billoo as the principal opened a drawer and took out some torn pages which I recognized at once.

'This is it; this is what the boy was reading' the principal said handing out the pages to my guardian.

There was a solemn expression for about ten seconds on the face of Billoo. He seemed to be deeply moved by what he was seeing; it was as if he couldn't believe that I had done such a grave job at school.

'Quite bad' he murmured. His acting was superb; the principal couldn't guess him one bit.

'Yes,' said the principal, 'and my colleagues say that there are some immoral things written apart from the offensive photos.'

What the hell? He couldn't see it for himself; his colleagues said? Was it that he didn't have much time to read these things, or was it that he couldn't understand anything but for the photos? Maybe it was the second case; don't forget that there were rumours of him being a peon previously.

'Arjun, I didn't expect this from you' said Billoo turning his face to me for the first time. 'What made you do this?'

I kept mum. The principal, meanwhile, seemed to be intriguingly enjoying the situation.

'Tell me, why did you do this?'

'Sorry uncle' I said looking at the floor. It was shiny-reddish white marble stones of the latest design contributed for the floorboard.

'Sorry won't do', said Billoo raising his voice to that of intense grief. 'I need explanation.'

'Sorry.'

'Rubbish man... err Arjun. You were reading nude things? Enjoying stripped photos of hot women? Ask the principal sir if he had done anything like this in his schooldays. Had you, sir?' said Billoo turning to the principal.

'I... no... never, never in my life' said the principal.

'See, and that's why he is the principal of such a big and reputed school' said Billoo. I saw the principal's face by the corner of my eye; there was a genuine smile.

'Sorry uncle, I wouldn't repeat this' I said.

'You shouldn't be allowed to. I think you should be expelled. Right, professor?'

'W-what? No, I don't think so.'

'Then you're thinking wrong, principal. Give him expulsion, I say' said Billoo with burning eyes. He was dealing with the situation with so much ferocity, yet with a touch of elegance.

'No, he could be spared' said the principal as if requesting.

'No sir, he is jeopardizing the atmosphere. I think he'll ruin the careers of other boys, and probably girls' said Billoo. 'This boy should be expelled from this school for the school's benefit... and maybe his own too.'

'What did you say?' asked the principal, puzzled.

'I said that he should be thrown away from the school. Reading porn things, oh... I can't stand this. Even I didn't do this at school. College is fine, don't you think so, principal?' said Billoo in an expert tone.

'W-what? Yes, college,' said the principal not able to find the suitable words, 'you get big enough at college.'

'Yeah... you see, Arjun. Even your principal sir says this all is fine at college, maybe he had done this too at college.'

'No, I never did,' said the principal in a low voice, 'some of my friends did though.'

'By the way what things were written in the pages, professor?' said Billoo in almost a teasing voice.

'I don't know... though there are some bad things written' said the principal.

'Like what?'

'Like ways of doing se- , I told you I don't know.'

'Never mind professor,' said Billoo.

'Arjun, never repeat this at school' interacted the principal with me for the first time.

'So what do you say, should we spare him?' asked Billoo.

'Right, I think the boy repents.'

'I don't think he does. He shouldn't be spared' said Billoo.

'No no, he should be. They are just kids, can't keep away from making mistakes. We should just teach, not just expel them. If we do, there are chances that they might deteriorate further' said the principal.

'I still don't agree professor' said Billoo.

'You should. He should be forgiven' said the principal.

'You don't deserve to be this school's principal' said Billoo.

'What?' said the principal seeming offended.

'No offence made sir, but I think you are very lenient. You should be cruel and harsh, you need to be a beast' said Billoo bantering the principal at an extreme level. It was just so phenomenal that he was doing it with so much ease without our principal realizing that he was being taunted.

'No, schools don't work out quite like that,' said the principal, 'that's why our school is the best. It's simply because of a principal like me.'

'Oh, as is the school, so is the principal', said Billoo. 'Unbelievable.'

'Thanks' said the principal blushing at my guardian's comment.

'Sir, I thank you for forgiving my mistake' I said.

'No problems mate,' said Billoo before principal could say anything. 'The professor realizes that your mistake isn't such a grave one.'

'I didn't say that,' interrupted the principal, 'I just said that he should be given a second chance.'

'Yeah... similar stuff' said Billoo. 'Should we leave then, sir?'

'I think so.'

'Thanks sir,' said Billoo rising off his chair and proceeding towards the principal. And he went and hugged him; yes, Billoo engulfed the principal in a deep hug.

'W-what the hell do you think you are doing?'

'Just thanking you, sir. Not many principals would've spared a boy who was caught appreciating nude contents' said Billoo.

'Nothing, it really is nothing,' said the principal, 'and I'm benevolent, you see.'

'Yeah... and a fool too' said Billoo in an extremely low voice so that I could only hear.

'See you again' said Billoo and both of us proceeded towards the exit. I didn't want to leave the room. It was so much cooler and cozier here.

'You handled it perfectly man' I said as we showed our thumbs-up to Pranav and Chinku for a fine meeting with the *professor*.

'Nothing, it really is nothing' said Billoo mimicking the principal's voice. It was so real that for a moment I thought that it was the principal himself who was speaking. Then, realizing it was another intriguing part of Billoo's multipurpose personality, we both shared a quiet laugh.

It was about after fifteen minutes that Pranav and Chinku emerged back to the waiting room where I was asking Billoo about his future plans.

'Great dude,' said Pranav ecstatic with joy, 'Chinku was superb.'

'Shhh... keep your voice down mate' said Chinku.

'Sorry... but Chinku did it perfectly well' said Pranav leaning closer.

'So did Billoo,' I said, 'thank you so much both of you. You saved our asses from getting burnt.'

'No problems mate,' said Chinku. 'Anytime you wish, but make sure that the next time we come here there is a different reason. This principal gave me a headache on immoral proposition.'

'You ought to get a treat,' said Pranav, 'both of you. Where do you prefer?'

'No, we just did it because we are your friends, though we are much older' said Chinku.

'Of course we're friends, but that doesn't mean we can't have a blast tonight. You saved our *asses,* don't you understand?' said Pranav.

'Okay, if you insist so much, tomorrow. Tonight I'm busy' said Billoo.

'Whenever, thanks man, you both did a great job,' said Pranav. 'We've been spared for reading porn things in a school where students get expulsion for sitting on the chair.'

'Chairs are where students are supposed to seat, isn't it?' asked a bewildered Billoo.

'Yeah...it's only that the chair belonged to the principal' I said.

# Epilogue

Well, was my school life really like hell? Indeed it wasn't... it was because of the school that I befriended so many dudes who had a great influence on my life. I don't have a clue about my future and that's bad considering the current atmosphere being highly competitive. But then, who cares? Maybe the world will fall tonight.

My school did suck every drop of my bottomless red blood. Who says only the elders in a family have tensions? We have, and nothing less. We've to get good marks in exams, we have to build a future for ourselves, and we have to fabricate our personality....

Only this much? Noah, there are loads more...

We've to find our friends; friends who are made for life. We've to make our girlfriends (it'll be fantastic if you can carry on with a girlfriend for a year though), and again we've to resist the high-school years which are devilish at times.

But, as I've already told you that I respect my school for the friends it has bestowed to me.

I've many friends, and all are of a different breed...

Some are like me; average in everything, yet love anything that has to do with the betterment of one's existence.

Some are good-looking, fine in academics, and rich in girlfriends; yet, they have nothing to boast about.

Some are big dudes who are always ready to fight for any reason; yet, they talk to me as if they are the mellowest from their hearts.

Some are chain smokers, and heavy drinkers; yet, they don't ask me once to live like them.

But there's something common about all of them- they love me, and I love them...

This book is not meant for intellectuals; they might find it dull and out of resources. But this is meant for those who are my kind- run of the mill in everything they do.

Now, I'll talk about what happened to me after the events that I've mentioned. Pranav and I gave a great treat to the dudes who had saved us from the school authorities. My schooldays continued to be exceedingly boring, but my friendship kept on reaching new parameters. My relation with Shikha has reached a level that both of us are jovial about. And above all, I'm still not labouring hard enough for keeping my future on the right track.

But I'm hopeful; hopeful that someday I might be of some use for this big, bulky and yet lovable nation. Maybe a day will come that I'll cherish for what I'm; you've to keep thinking this way or you'll fail at your very first hurdle.

Did you enjoy the stay with me and my friends?

Maybe yes; I thank you for that.

Maybe no, and I thank you even more. You might abhor this book if you are above me academically or fundamentally and I'm happy for you. You're the kind of person that can make this country reach the pinnacle of sensation.

I think I've been unable to put my life in a stylish and an attractive way, but that's the way it is. My existence on this planet is neither stylish, nor attractive. How many times will I have to remind you that this is a common experience of an absolute commoner?

My family is my life...

My friends are my family...

My parents are my friends...

And my life is my parents...

That's as simple as my life is...

Love everyone around you and see the difference, the great people say.

Love yourself and see the difference, I don't know who says...

Though my school has been the hell of my life, I still want to have three cheers for the boring place...

HIP HIP HURRAY...

HIP HIP HURRAY...

HIP HIP HURRAY...

After all, this is the place that made me a man. It's not that I was a woman before that; I was just a boy who had limited ambitions.

One needs to get out to the world to know what he really is; being inside doesn't felicitate the potential...

So get out, see the world and love yourself... and if possible, love your school. I don't want people to loathe their nurturing-place just as I've done in the last eighteen months or so.

But then, you'll have to agree that there weren't too many options. I just couldn't, somehow, afford to develop a liking for my school.

I've so many things to say, but then this'll never end... and my mother wishes this book to end fast, so that I can get off it and start preparing for my exams which *might*, I say just *might*, decide my future.

Great have been the times that I've spent with you, and I've loved every bit of it. There are chances that you haven't loved any bit of it, but then I'm glad that at least you dared to finish off this tome... or am I wrong, have you directly skipped to the *epilogue* part?

It's time for me and my friends to depart... but who knows when next I might be knocking on your doors again. Surely there isn't another school to attend, but who knows what is lurking in their way in the future.

I hated my school, for the school it was...

And I loved my school, for what it provided me...

# Index